BOOK FOUR
EQUINE BUSINESS MANAGEMENT

Essential Equine Studies

BOOK FOUR

EQUINE BUSINESS MANAGEMENT

JULIE BREGA

J. A. Allen

LONDON

ACKNOWLEDGEMENTS

Thanks to Naomi Beveridge and Emma Hannant for their assistance with checking content in Chapters 1, 2, 3, 4 and 5 and Erica Taylor for assistance with Chapter 6.

ISBN 978 0 85131 972 8

J.A. Allen
Clerkenwell House
Clerkenwell Green
London EC1R 0HT

J.A. Allen is an imprint of Robert Hale Limited

www.allenbooks.co.uk

A catalogue record for this book is available from the British Library

Design by Judy Linard
Edited by Martin Diggle

Printed in China

CONTENTS

LIST OF TABLES

INTRODUCTION

Most equestrian business proprietors have a detailed knowledge of horses and are dedicated to their work. Most people involved in the equestrian industry put in very long hours, often in unfavourable conditions. Hard though they may work, however, there are many who take only a little (if any) interest in the financial aspects of the business.

Often, businesses fail or fall into dire financial straits because of poor business planning and money management. There is often the assumption that, because the riding school has large cash takings on a Saturday, 'everything must be all right'. This, combined with a 'head in the sand' attitude, can lead to problems.

Financial matters tend to be left to the book-keeper and accountant because, apart from a lack of knowledge of such issues, the equestrian business proprietor does not have the time to spend doing all of the bookwork. It is, of course, an excellent idea to employ a skilled book-keeper and accountant as the proprietor is then free to create income through teaching, schooling, etc. However, a basic understanding of the principles of book-keeping and business planning may lead to more efficient organization of money matters which, in turn, will improve the chances of making a profit.

When running any sort of equestrian business, one should aim, as far as practicable, to be a business manager as well as a yard manager and/or (for example) instructor.

At this point, we should perhaps consider what is meant by 'equestrian business' for the purposes of this book. The core equestrian businesses in the UK are based around actual riding in some form, the most prevalent being riding schools, livery yards and various types of training centres. However, the 'equestrian industry' obviously extends beyond these core elements, to include more specialized areas such as competition yards, racing yards and studs and the 'service' areas such as farriery, tack shops, etc. Although the core aims and activities of these businesses differ substantially from one to another, there are many aspects of business administration and practice that are common to all. For example, employers have a statutory duty of care to their employees, which apply whether the employee is a groom in a livery yard, a farrier's apprentice or the odd-job man at a stud farm. Similarly, for all employers, some knowledge of business planning and financial management will be necessary if they are to remain as employers in any business for any length of time.

Because these tenets of running a business apply 'across the board', in writing this book, we have not restricted ourselves to some arbitrary list of what constitutes 'equestrian businesses', but have endeavoured to offer practical examples throughout the text from a range of equestrian business activities.

This book aims to provide managers of equestrian businesses with a basic understanding of the fundamentals of business management. It is intended to enable you to make informed decisions in conjunction with professionals such as your solicitor and accountant.

It should be noted that legislation concerning business management and employment law is changing continually and it is beyond the scope of this book to explain these complex and varying topics in full. You are therefore strongly recommended to ask a solicitor or accountant for specialist advice on legal and financial matters.

The information provided within this book applies to the United Kingdom and is correct at the end of writing.

> *If you are studying the information from outside the UK, certain topics will be completely different from those pertaining in your own country, and some of the information may be irrelevant to your circumstances. Try, where possible, to find out whether your national laws and practices have any broad equivalents to those mentioned in this book and relate them, as appropriate, to the details given.*

CHAPTER I

BUSINESS PLANNING

The aims and objectives of this chapter are to explain:

- The terms used in business and financial management.
- The main aspects to consider before deciding to set up a business.
- The forms a business can take.
- How to prepare a business plan.
- How to prepare a cash flow forecast and profit and loss forecast.
- The options available in terms of initial finance for the business.

Many people would, at some time, like to work for themselves. What better than to be able to develop your hobby into a business that will provide an income for you and your family? There are definitely many attractions to running your own business; equally, there are many pitfalls and disadvantages. This chapter considers the positive and negative aspects of running a business and outlines the main requirements for setting up the business.

To help your understanding we start by explaining some of the terms used in financial management.

GLOSSARY OF TERMS

Accruals	Services/goods used but not yet paid for – shown on the balance sheet as current liabilities, e.g. a visit by the vet that has not yet been invoiced, or electricity used before it is invoiced.
Annual accounts	The recorded summary of all financial aspects of the business for the financial year, prepared by the accountant and presented to HM Customs and Revenue. They normally comprise the balance sheet and trading and profit and loss accounts.
Assets	Items owned by the business that have a measurable money value. They are divided into:

     a. **Fixed assets** – premises, equipment, vehicles, etc. that are retained for a long time and are not generally for re-sale – they are used to generate revenue.

     b. **Current assets** – short-term assets that will not last longer than one year, for example stock, outstanding debtors, cash and prepayments (items/services paid for but not yet received).

Audit

A process carried out by an independent accountant (an auditor) on a company's annual accounts. It is a statutory requirement that the accounts of large limited companies with an annual turnover of more than the specified threshold are audited. There is no requirement for a sole trader's accounts to be audited.

Balance sheet

A statement of a business's assets and liabilities. The figures on the balance sheet represent the true value of the company at that point in time.

Business plan

An analysis of the nature of the business and a forecast of expected business activities. It is designed to persuade financial backers to invest in the business.

Capital

Money contributed to the business by the owner and therefore owed by the business to the owner. This may be described as:

a. Total value of assets less total external liabilities, (money owed to banks, building societies and other creditors), or

b. Net capital employed (working capital); current assets less current liabilities. Used to keep the business working and to pay off creditors.

Capital expenditure

Money used to buy fixed assets – as shown on the balance sheet and depreciated on the profit and loss account.

Cash book

Record of payments and receipts whether made by cash, cheque or credit card.

Cash flow

The process of total cash coming in and going out of the business over a period of time.

Cash purchases

Purchases of goods paid for immediately by cash, cheque or credit card.

Cash sales

Sales for which payment is made immediately either by cash, cheque or credit card.

Cost of sales

A term used in the trading account to represent cost of

materials or items used which, when taken from your sales figure, gives you the gross profit – after adjusting for opening and closing stock.

Credit   The supply of goods or services without immediate payment. This is usually subject to a pre-agreed timescale.

Credit purchases   Purchases paid for within an agreed time limit.

Credit sales   Sales to customers which should be paid for within the time specified on the invoice.

Credit account   Account held by a trusted customer invoiced, perhaps monthly, and paid in arrears.

Creditor   A supplier to whom money is owed.

Current liabilities See Accruals.

ITQ 1 Explain the following terms:

Accruals.

Capital expenditure.

Capital.

ITQ 2 What would be shown on a balance sheet?

ITQ 3 When would a company's annual accounts have to be audited?

Debtor Someone who owes money (in our context, a client/customer who owes money to the business).

Depreciation The cost of using a fixed asset over a period of time; essentially, the decrease in value of the asset over the period, which may be caused by wear and tear (equipment eventually wears out), obsolescence (after some time you may no longer be able to get parts to repair a piece of equipment), inadequacy (the business might outgrow the equipment over a period of time), or simply the passage of time (a 10-year lease on premises only has any value for the 10 years in which it is in operation).

Direct costs Expenses such as materials which vary according to services offered/sales achieved, e.g. the amount of feed, hay and bedding used in a livery yard will be directly affected by the number of horses in the yard.

Drawings Amounts of money or goods taken out of the business for the owner's own use (applicable when operating as a sole trader only).

Dividend The share of profits paid by a limited company to its shareholders.

Facility A loan or overdraft provided by a bank to a business.

ITQ 4 Explain the following terms:

Fixed assets.

Current assets.

ITQ 5 What is a creditor?

Financial year The accounting year of the business; 12-month period shown in the profit and loss account.

Fiscal year HM Revenue and Customs operates on fiscal years from 6th April one year to 5th April of the next.

Fixed cost	See Overheads.
Gross profit	Equals sales figure (turnover) less purchases figure (direct costs – adjusted to take account of opening and closing stock), found on the trading account. It is the profit made before the deduction of overheads.
Indirect costs	See Overheads.
Liabilities	Debts or future commitments of the business. Long-term liabilities include capital, bank loan/mortgage, i.e. the means of purchasing the assets. Current liabilities are those debts to be paid within 12 months, for example creditors, overdraft and accruals, i.e. services used but not yet invoiced for.
Liquid asset	An asset which can be converted into cash very easily.
Net profit	Equals gross profit less expenses (overheads); found on the profit and loss account.
Overdraft	Extension of credit by bank on a current account.
Overheads	Expenses of the business. Most remain fixed regardless of turnover, for example rent, and may also be described as fixed or indirect costs. However, some, e.g. printing costs, will vary according to business activity.

ITQ 6 Explain the term depreciation.

ITQ 7 What is a dividend?

ITQ 8 What are drawings?

ITQ 9 Explain the following terms:

Debtor.

Cash flow.

Direct costs.

ITQ 10 Explain gross and net profit.

Gross profit:

Net profit:

ITQ 11 What are liabilities?

Petty cash book	The book used for recording all low-value purchases bought with money from the petty cash box and recorded on petty cash vouchers.
Profit and loss account	A statement showing sales, purchases, and profits (or losses) for an accounting period, normally one year.
Revenue expenditure	Expenditure on other than fixed assets. The day-to-day expenditure required to run the business.
Statement of account	Received from bank or from a supplier; shows all relevant financial transactions and finishes with the amount you owe or are owed.
Stock	Goods used in some form for resale. In a dealer's yard, horses; in a tack shop, tack.
Trading account	Summary of sales and purchases for any period, usually one year, showing gross profits.
Turnover	The total sales for the year (less any returns).
Variable costs	See Direct costs.

ITQ 12 What are overheads?

ITQ 13 Give two other terms that have the same meaning as overheads.

ITQ 14 Explain the following terms:

Fiscal year.

Financial year.

PLANNING AN EQUESTRIAN BUSINESS

The equestrian industry covers a wide spectrum of horse-related activities, the majority of which are enjoying expansion as more people turn to the horse in their pursuit of pleasure. Running an equestrian business can be very rewarding – it can also be a major financial and administrative challenge!

Many businesses operate for love of the horse, but this on its own is not enough – for a business to survive it must at worst cover its costs, but should ideally make a profit.

Good planning will improve any business's chances of survival. Many skills other than equestrian ones are needed when in businesses related to horses. This is true whether running one's own yard or acting as yard manager for an employer.

REALITIES TO CONSIDER

Research shows that approximately 85 per cent of businesses fail within the first 5 years. Horse-related businesses have a tendency to change hands frequently and often fail because of a lack of initial planning.

Problems facing equestrian business include:

- Getting established.
- Consolidating the business once established.
- Limited financial resources.
- The labour-intensive nature of dealing with horses.
- Very high costs associated with keeping horses.

- Seasonality – for example, with a riding school, unless an indoor school is available, earnings drop in the winter months. In the case of a hunting and/or point-to-point yard, the summer months will prove quiet.
- Coping with expansion.

Although they may have many useful attributes, equestrian business managers might lack skills in the following areas:

- Financial planning and record-keeping.
- Staff management and training.
- Marketing.
- Public relations.
- The law and insurance.

Specialists may have to be consulted in these areas.

Good plans are fundamental to both survival and long-term profitability. These plans include market research, the business plan, cash flow forecast and profit and loss budget – factors that will be addressed in this chapter.

MARKET RESEARCH AND PRACTICAL PLANNING

Market research is the starting point in establishing the viability of any business idea and is simply to do with 'finding out' – it need not be an expensive process. The process involves discovering the answers to the following questions:

- Do you possess the necessary personal qualities to make the business a success?
- What services will you offer?
- What are the goals and objectives of the business?
- Who will be your clients?
- Why will they be your clients?
- Where will your clients come from?
- Who are your competitors?
- What premises will you use? Can you get planning permission?
- What will be the scale of the business?
- What form will the business take?
- Will you need to employ staff?
- What are the principal risks faced by the business?
- What can be done to minimize these risks?

Let's examine these matters in more detail.

Requisite Personal Qualities

Running your own business requires certain personal qualities. Deciding whether you possess them requires a degree of self-analysis. The requisite personal qualities include:

- Motivation.
- A positive attitude.
- Energy.
- Initiative.
- Self-confidence.
- Determination.
- Persistence.
- A realistic approach.
- Good judgement.
- Self-discipline.
- Mental and physical good health.
- Appropriate knowledge.

Answering the following questions will help you decide whether you have what it takes to stand a chance of running a successful business. Could you:

- Work harder?
- Work for longer hours?
- Forego perks such as holidays?
- Solve problems?
- Think up new ideas and make them work?
- Handle several different things at the same time without getting confused?
- Get on well with people (even awkward ones)?
- Accept expert advice?

And:

- Do you know your subject and market thoroughly?

- A supportive family is a bonus. Will your family encourage and support you? Are they happy to be involved and take the risks associated with running your own business? Is there any member of the family, particularly your spouse, who is against the idea?

> **ITQ 15** List some of the problems that might be faced when establishing an equestrian business.

> **ITQ 16** List some of the qualities you might consider about yourself in deciding whether to set up a business.

Services to Offer

The broader the range of services offered, the larger the potential clientele will be. Some businesses specialize in specific aspects of equestrianism whilst others provide an all-round service. Services offered may include a combination of the following:

- **Livery.** Full, working, grass or do-it-yourself (DIY).

- **Exercise and schooling.** May be part of a full livery arrangement.

- **Breaking and training.** Only to be undertaken by skilled staff.

- **Instruction.** Group and private lessons, novices ranging from young children and nervous mums through to inexperienced men. More experienced riders will require instruction to a higher level. Riding for the disabled is an important and worthwhile aspect, but requires additional skills of the instructor and also extra helpers. Further information can be obtained from the Riding for the Disabled website www.rda.org.uk.

- **Trekking/hacking.** Good countryside with minimal roadwork is desirable for hacking and essential for trekking.

- **Hire of horses/ponies.** For hunting, shows, Pony/Riding Club rallies, etc.

- **Competition training.** For horse and rider combinations.

- **Exam training.** In preparation for professional qualifications. (Some form of accommodation arrangements for students may well be needed.)

- **Stable management instruction.** Courses of various lengths, lectures, demonstrations, etc.

- **Dealing.** Buying and selling horses and ponies.

- **Clipping and trimming.** This may involve travel to clients.

- **Hiring out facilities.** Manège, indoor school, showjumps and cross-country course.

- **Specialist spheres:**
    - Driving.
    - Polo.
    - Showing.
    - Lecture/demonstrations by renowned competition riders.
    - Horse transportation.
    - Breeding – stud facilities may include stallion services, mares taken for foaling, etc.

- Racing.
- Hosting competitions.
- Tack shop – perhaps also selling horse/pet feedstuff.
- Rehabilitation and therapeutic facilities.

The Goals and Objectives of the Business

At the outset, the objectives of the business should be defined, and ways of achieving them planned. The business idea will need to be well thought out to ensure that you are providing the right service in the right place, at the right time, for the right price.

Try to offer:

The right service ⟶ High-quality livery, instruction, training, etc.

In the right place ⟶ Ideally, the location should suit the yard, (near centre of population with good riding countryside).

At the right time ⟶ When there is a demand, supply the service (e.g. hunter liveries).

For the right price ⟶ This does not mean cheap! Properly calculated fees, providing good value for money whilst still being profitable, are essential.

Prospective Clients

The clientele envisaged will influence your advertising campaign. Your clients will fall into some of the following categories:

- Professionals within the equestrian industry.
- Non-professionals.
- Male/female – young/old?
- Total beginner, novice, fairly competent.
- Competitive/non-competitive.
- Very keen/fairly keen/not that keen but want to 'have a go'.

There are many reasons why people ride horses:

- To improve professional qualifications.
- To achieve competitive goals.
- To take part in long-distance rides.
- For relaxation.
- To improve fitness.
- For fun and enjoyment.
- For the sense of achievement.
- To overcome fear and nervousness, and to gain confidence.

- To be with horses.
- To meet people.
- To enjoy the countryside.
- To go hunting.
- To enhance social status.
- Riding can be enjoyed by disabled and able-bodied people alike.

WHY WILL PEOPLE BE YOUR CLIENTS?

In any line of business, the chief reason why people become and, importantly, remain clients is quality of service. Offer a high quality in every aspect of the business including:

- The way in which the telephone is answered. Whoever answers the phone should be polite, cheerful and helpful.

- The way in which a visitor is greeted. All members of staff must be taught to offer assistance politely and to identify any persons found on the premises.

- The atmosphere and appearance of the premises. The staff should be well turned out, polite and friendly. The yard, office and stables (or other relevant areas) should be clean and tidy at all times.

- In businesses involving horses, the standard of horse care and stable management should be exemplary. The horses must look and feel well and be neatly turned out in clean, well-fitting and appropriate tack.

- Where instruction and training are involved, capable, well-qualified staff should be motivated to give their highest standard of teaching to all clients whether it is their first lesson of the day or their last; this is a very good reason for not overworking instructors or horses. Students and working pupils on the yard must be trained thoroughly and not treated as cheap labour.

- Customer care and general efficiency are qualities that must be evident at every level and in every aspect of yard/business management. Quality breeds success – people will associate the business with quality and will want to remain among the clientele.

WHERE WILL YOUR CLIENTS COME FROM?

This will depend upon various factors:

- Whether your business is near large towns and villages.

- Establishments offering specialist training (for example from a top competition trainer) will attract clients from further afield.

- The better the facilities or products on offer, the further people will travel.

- Depending on what is on offer, it may be necessary to provide/arrange accommodation in order to encourage people to travel long distances.

- Once your reputation as a high-class business is established, people will be happy to travel to reach you.

> **ITQ 17** Jot down the services you would like to offer if you were planning to set up an equestrian business.

Who are Your Competitors?

It is almost certain that you will face some sort of competition. Research along the following lines will be necessary:

1. Where are your competitors based? Will people travel to you even though your competitor is nearer to them? How are you going to encourage them to come to you?

2. Find out if a similar business to yours is proposing to set up in the same area. It may be possible to find out by asking the planning department in the local council offices. If the answer is yes, it may be appropriate to rethink your prospective location.

3. If a local business similar to the one you propose has recently closed down, try to find out why.

4. Obtain any informative literature offered by competitors or visit their yard discreetly and find out what services they offer and how much they charge.

Prospective Premises and Planning Permission

Very often, the family home and existing land and buildings are to be used for business purposes. Alternatively, a prospective entrepreneur sets out to buy or rent premises specifically with a view to running a business from there.

Before purchasing or renting a property, you must investigate the local authority's likely reaction to your application to run an equestrian business from there. The planning officers will visit the premises and discuss the planning implications with you.

In the UK, planning permission is needed for any development involving change of use, even though no structural alterations or additions may be required. Therefore a private residential property or farm must have approval from the planning authorities to be used for a riding school or similar activities.

An architect or chartered surveyor can help with planning matters, although their services are expensive. An architect will investigate a potential business premises, obtain planning permission, estimate costs, draw up plans, prepare contracts and supervise building work to completion. Architects also advise on structural alterations and fire and health and safety regulations. Surveyors can advise on the structural condition of premises and the planning requirements for the adaptation of existing buildings.

Should planning permission be refused, the applicant has the right to appeal. Ultimately, the appeal could be made to the Secretary of State for the Environment and this may involve a public inquiry.

When considering a planning application, the authorities take into account:

- The suitability of the site.

- The existence of any development plans and restrictions in that locality.

- The impact on amenities and the character of the area.

- Changes in the volume and type of traffic, access and road safety.

- Aesthetic appearance of buildings and materials to be used.

- Drainage – the effects of any extra burden on mains water and sewerage.

- The possibility of job creation (most areas are keen to reduce their unemployment figures).

- The effects on the landscape and wildlife.

- Noise, pollution and any other associated nuisances.

Your planning application should address all of these points. Attach reports you may have commissioned, or research to back up any statements you make in support of your application.

All building works are subject to building regulations. The architect will obtain the relevant forms and organize meetings and approval with the local building control officer.

When considering the purchase of premises, various further points need to be taken into account.

- Location – this should be suitable for the nature of the business, for example, a trekking centre will need vast areas of countryside while a racing yard will need gallops and relatively good access to racecourses.

- Access – the better the motorway and main road links, the easier it is for clients to reach the business.

- Centres of population – riding schools in particular need to be situated close to large towns in order to provide the necessary volume of clients.

- Reputation – if buying an existing business, find out whether it has a good or bad reputation. This helps you to plan your business idea and marketing strategy and should be taken into account when negotiating a price.

The Scale of the Business

To a certain extent this is dependent upon:

- The size of the premises and the amount of land available if using existing land and buildings.

- Any restrictions imposed, for example by planning authorities.

- Services offered.

- The number and variety of types of horses and ponies kept.

- The number of staff employed.

ITQ 18 List some of the things that a client might consider about how your business is run when deciding whether to use you or a competitor:

ITQ 19 Why do you need planning permission to set up an equestrian business from home, even if no building work is required?

The Form the Business Will Take

This should be discussed with experts such as the accountant, bank manager and solicitor.

There are three basic forms of business: sole trader, partnership and limited company.

SOLE TRADER

A sole trader is an individual trading under a business name. For example Nicola Smith trading as (often expressed as T/A) 'The Equestrian Centre'. The business is wholly owned by one individual who is liable for all debts of that business.

Advantages	This is a simple and flexible form of business which is easily set up. The proprietor receives all of the profits and is their own boss.
Disadvantages	The owner of the business is totally liable for all losses (unlimited liability). In some circumstances two classes of National Insurance Contributions may have to be paid but some social security benefits may be lost. There is no continuity on death. This means that the business ceases to exist if the proprietor dies. The deceased's estate will, however, be liable for any business debts.

The other forms of business are generally owned by more than one person.

PARTNERSHIP

A partnership is usually formed when one person has insufficient capital, experience or expertise to run the business successfully on their own.

Partnerships are governed by the Partnership Act 1890. A partnership is owned by at least two, and not usually more than twenty individuals. **Full partners** are personally liable for a share of the partnership's debts and would have to part with personal possessions if necessary to meet obligations under the partnership. A partnership can also have **limited partners** in which case it would also have to comply with the Limited Partnership Act 1907. Limited partners are not personally liable for a share of the partnership's debts. A limited partner's losses are limited to the value of the capital he or she has invested in the partnership. Limited partners cannot take part in running the business and are sometimes consequently known as **'sleeping partners'**. All of the partners cannot be limited partners.

Advantages	The workload and responsibilities are generally shared. Partners generally bring a wider range of skills than those of the sole trader. More capital may be available.
Disadvantages	Partners are 'jointly and severally' liable for the whole amount of debts incurred by the other(s) – each may be held liable for the total debt, even if they had no knowledge of it. One person does not have sole control. All profits are shared. The liability for debts is unlimited.

LIMITED COMPANY

A limited company is a business registered with Companies House as a public or private limited company under the Companies Acts (including those of

1985 and 1989). The business is owned by shareholders and managed by directors. The shareholders' liability in respect of the business's debts is limited either to the value of their shares or to the amount they have guaranteed to cover in the event of the business being wound up.

A public limited company:

- Has an authorized share capital of at least £50,000.
- Has at least two shareholders – there is no maximum number.
- May offer its shares to the public at large on the Stock Exchange.
- Must have a name ending in 'public limited company' or 'plc'.

A private limited company:

- Can have an authorized share capital of less than £50,000.
- May have only one shareholder.
- May not offer shares to the public at large.

Most equestrian businesses formed as limited companies will be private limited companies. Both private and public limited companies are governed by the Companies Acts 1985 and 1989. The 1989 Act makes amendments to the 1985 Act – both Acts are still in force.

Advantages	The company has its own identity, distinct from that of its directors. The directors are not personally liable for debts incurred by the company. Shareholders' liability is limited. There is continuity on death – shares in the company remain the property of the deceased's estate.
Disadvantages	The start-up process is quite complicated and there are many restrictions and formalities. Accounts are available to the public. It is essential to discuss company formation with a solicitor.

STATUTORY ACCOUNTING REQUIREMENTS

There are different statutory accounting requirements for small and medium-sized private limited companies.

Small company

A small company is defined as:

- Having an annual turnover of £5.6 million or less.
- The balance sheet total must be £2.8 million or less.
- The company must have an average of 50 employees or less.

Medium company

A medium company is defined as:

- Having an annual turnover of £22.8 million or less.
- The balance sheet total must be £5.6 million or less.
- The company must have an average of 250 employees or less.

ITQ 20 List two advantages of operating as a sole trader:

1.

2.

ITQ 21 List two advantages of operating as a partnership:

1.

2.

The Need to Employ Staff

Having established what form the business will take you must consider the staffing requirements. If staff are needed:

- How many?

- What tasks will they perform?

- What qualifications and skills will they need?

- What training will they need?

- Who will provide this training?

- Will it be in-house or elsewhere?

- Where will you find them?

- What will you pay them?

- Will there be other perks, for example keep of horse, food and/or accommodation?

- Have you budgeted for this?

Principal Business Risks

Equestrian businesses are exposed to many risks which, without sufficient attention, can cause the downfall of the enterprise. These risks include:

- High overheads, such as mortgage/rent on equestrian property, rates on buildings and so on.

- The very high cost of keeping horses.

- Loss of use of animals for reasons such as lameness or the outbreak of an infectious or contagious ailment.

- Seasonal variances – most establishments have a busy season when income is high, but during the 'off-season' income is greatly reduced. For example a riding school without an indoor school or good quality all-weather surface will suffer a loss of earnings during the winter.

MINIMIZING THE RISKS

- Try to reduce overheads wherever practical.

- Try to minimize the costs of keeping horses without making false economies. For example look for good-quality feed and hay at competitive prices and try to negotiate a discount. Buying hay and straw directly off the field is usually cheaper than buying barn-stored hay.

- Try to prevent illness and lameness in horses. Do not overwork riding school mounts. Keep shoeing, rasping teeth, worming and vaccinations up to date.

- Try to budget for any slack periods and think of means of earning money during these times. For example, if riding lessons are disrupted whilst an all-weather arena is being laid, consider offering a course in stable management.

- If relevant to your type of business, look into the cost-effectiveness of building an indoor school. Bear in mind, however, that by the time you have considered all costs of purchase, rates and so on, you have to run a very large and busy establishment to make it worthwhile.

ITQ 22 Why might you decide to set up your business as a limited company?

PREPARING THE BUSINESS PLAN

Once all of the aspects of running a business detailed so far in this chapter have been considered, you will be able to make an informed decision whether to go ahead. If you do decide to proceed, one of the first things you will need to do is produce a business plan.

The business plan helps to ensure that the business has the potential to be profitable – a point that will be important in any bank manager's opinion when considering the loan of money. It also ensures that the business owner fully understands the extent of all financial commitments and has researched the market to help maximize the business potential. Any problems may be identified early and dealt with before they affect the business.

DRAFT AND STRUCTURE

The business plan is a lengthy and important document so care and time need to go into its preparation. Gather all relevant information and figures before trying to write it. Decide on the structure of the plan – work out what headings you need and in what order. Most banks can provide pre-prepared business plan forms in hard copy or on-line as part of their Small Business Advice Service, so it may be useful to obtain one for guidance, even if you feel that minor changes are needed to represent your business accurately. The business plan should be realistic, workable, clear, well presented and properly documented.

Once you are happy with the final draft of your business plan, take copies and present it in a neat document file or ring binder along with the projected profit and loss budget and cash flow forecast. If you have pre-arranged to visit the bank (a good idea from everyone's point of view) the business plan and other figures should be presented to the manager a few days in advance, so it can be studied before your meeting.

Suggested Headings and Format

A number of headings are required for the business plan. A suggested format includes the following:

1. **Synopsis.** An introductory page which can be read in a short space of time, outlining the key points of the business plan.

2. **Introduction.** Give the business name and details of any logo to be used. State what form the business is to take; whether sole trader, partnership or limited company. Introduce the business with a general outline of what you intend to do and how the business will develop.

3. **Personal details.** Give your full name, address, date of birth and details of professional qualifications. Describe briefly what previous experience you have had and why you wish to run your own business. Lenders are always happier dealing with people with a good track record. Never be dishonest about any of your previous financial failures or mistakes – the banks have ways of finding out before they lend you their money.

4. **Objectives of the business.** Outline the objectives for the different areas of the business and describe what you want out of the business and over what period of time, both short-term (up to 1 year) and medium-term

(1–5 years). You could also try to provide an outline prediction of the long-term future of the business.

5. **Services to be offered.** Explain the nature of all services you will offer.

6. **Marketing.** Give accurate details of the market (customers – who, where and why). Calculate the cost of your marketing campaign. Give information about where and when you will advertise.

7. **Premises, horses, equipment available.** What is available, what you will need and how much they will cost.

8. **Personnel requirements.** The staff you will need, their qualifications and/or experience and what you will pay them.

5. **Record (book-keeping) system to be used.** State how you intend keeping the books (for details, see Chapter 2) and which book-keeper (if any) and accountant you will use.

10. **Financial details.** Give details of all assets, their value and life expectancy. The bank will be interested in your collateral, i.e. what security you can pledge as a guarantee for repayment of the money. You may need to provide some form of security if you wish to borrow money.

11. **Expected costs.** Prepare a list of costs, detailing how often they are incurred and when they have to be paid.

Also prepare and attach to the plan:

- A cash flow forecast.
- A projected profit and loss forecast.

(A method of preparing these documents is explained further on in the chapter).

These should cover the first 12 months of business. Always include realistic living expenses. Explain how you arrived at these figures and how you anticipate the business will develop financially, bearing in mind that initially income is low and outgoings are high. A simple breakdown of these figures should be prepared. The advice of the accountant may be sought to help with preparation of financial forecasts.

Other information provided should include the name of the business's solicitor and whether the business is registered for Value Added Tax (VAT) or not. The question of whether the business should be registered for VAT is an important one which you should discuss with your accountant. VAT registration is covered later in this chapter.

Also mention insurance policies and any other relevant information.

THE BOOK-KEEPING SYSTEM

As you need to decide which book-keeping system you will use at this planning stage, we will now look briefly at the main systems available. The exact method of keeping records is covered in Chapter 2.

When deciding how to keep the records it is important to consider simplicity and usefulness. Complicated systems deter most busy people from attempting to keep the bookwork up to date. Records, whether containing financial information or other details, such as feed charts, should:

1. Serve a definite purpose which can be easily identified to those keeping the record.
2. Be accurate.
3. Be easy (simple and relatively quick) to complete.
4. Be kept up to date.
5. Be easily stored and readily accessible.

The system chosen must be useful to the particular type of business without being excessively time-consuming. There are many book-keeping systems to choose from – most fit into one of the following categories:

1. **Analysed cash book.** This is the simplest method and forms the basis for the proprietary off-the-shelf systems. A large bound cash book can be bought to provide an effective but straightforward method of recording all cash received and payments made. Such books are available already ruled into a number of columns on each page and the columns can be headed to

suit your particular requirements. The columns on the left are used to record receipts and those on the right to record payments.

2. **Off-the-shelf systems.** There are several off-the-shelf proprietary systems such as Simplex or Kalamazoo which take some of the repetitive work out of the analysed cash book. Your book-keeper or accountant should be able to recommend a suitable one.

3. **Double entry method.** This is more complex and requires setting up and maintaining a manual double entry book-keeping system. It is only really necessary when your business becomes very large and even under these circumstances a better alternative would be to use a computer system.

4. **Computer systems.** Whatever the size or nature of the business, every book-keeping procedure can be computerized. There is a huge range of accounting software systems available, making the task of keeping records simpler and quicker. A computer software dealer will offer advice on suitable systems – there are systems specially designed for the specific requirements of equestrian businesses.

The chief advantage of using a computerised book-keeping system is that data are only keyed into the computer once. The computer then does everything with the figure that needs to be done. This greatly reduces the amount of time spent updating records. Some systems go right through to preparing the final accounts and will ask for any missing figures needed. These final accounts can be asked for every day if required, all at the push of a single key. Thus, time and effort can be saved provided the proprietor and staff have the knowledge needed to operate the computer.

You can learn computer skills on-line via e-learning or by attending evening classes at your local college. The software dealer will guide the computer operator initially and most companies offer an after-sales advice service.

ITQ 23 List the main headings that you would need in a business plan:

ITQ 24 What is an analysed cash book?

List of Costs

Costs that might be incurred include:

- **Set-up costs** – one-off costs associated with starting the business, such as:
  - Premises.
  - Alterations to premises.
  - Equipment.
  - Horses.
  - Tack, rugs, etc.

- **For premises**
  - Rent (usually payable monthly or quarterly).
  - Business rates (payable monthly/quarterly or annually).
  - Electricity (usually paid quarterly).
  - Water rates (usually paid annually or monthly).
  - Telephone (paid quarterly).
  - Maintenance costs (monthly allowance).
  - Buildings and contents insurance (usually payable monthly or annually).

- **For staff**
  - Wages (paid weekly or monthly).
  - Pay As You Earn (PAYE) and National Insurance Contributions (NICs) (usually paid monthly).
  - Employers' Liability Insurance (compulsory insurance for employers, usually paid annually or monthly).
  - Training costs.

- **Costs associated with keeping horses**
  - Feed.
  - Hay.
  - Straw/other bedding.
  - Veterinary fees.
  - Shoeing.
  - Insurance.
  - Tack repairs.
  - Tack replacement.

- **Other costs**
  - Public Liability Insurance (compulsory insurance – usually payable annually).
  - Professional fees (solicitor and accountant).
  - Motor expenses (including insurance costs, maintenance costs and fuel for any vehicles used by the business).
  - Equipment maintenance.
  - Office supplies (stationery, postage and printing).
  - Drawings (for sole traders) or salary – how much will you need to take out of the business each month to live on?
  - Licence fees.

– Interest on loans or overdrafts and bank charges.

– Advertising.

– Ad-hoc expenses (including outside instructors, judges, competition entries, etc.).

Once you have established all of the costs that might be incurred by the business and the frequency at which resulting bills will be due for payment, you will then be able to calculate your forecast of each cost.

REGISTERING FOR VALUE ADDED TAX

If your business is based in the UK you have to decide at this planning stage whether or not to register for value added tax (VAT). However, a business has no choice on whether to register for VAT once its annual turnover exceeds the threshold set by the Government – although it may, in special circumstances, as outlined shortly, ask to be exempted from VAT.

In effect, by registering for VAT, the business becomes an unpaid tax collector, required to collect tax on sales against which VAT is payable and to pay this over to HM Revenue and Customs periodically. Being VAT-registered will involve extra paperwork which must be kept correctly and submitted on time. Penalties are charged if the paperwork is insufficient or returns or payments are not made on time. The main disadvantage in being VAT-registered is that in charging VAT your prices will almost certainly be higher than smaller competitors who are not registered. This can be a serious drawback for small businesses.

Registering for VAT does, however, have advantages to some businesses. If registered for VAT, you may be able to claim back the VAT you have paid on goods and services purchased.

Do you know what the current VAT threshold is? If not, check with your local HM Revenue and Customs.

Date: VAT threshold: £

HM Revenue and Customs might consider exempting a business from VAT if the business's sales are all zero-rated and there is no VAT to collect. It this was the case, it might seem beneficial to be registered – you wouldn't have to charge VAT but could claim it back on all your purchases. However, if the amount you could reclaim was fairly low, you might prefer not to have to comply with the paperwork requirements of HM Revenue and Customs.

Some businesses, even if their turnover exceeded the VAT threshold, would be ineligible to register for VAT. This would be the case if the business's sales were all exempt from VAT. In this case, the business could not register for VAT and could not therefore claim back the VAT it had paid on purchases. An equine insurance company is one example.

If only part of the business's sales are exempt from VAT, the VAT-exempt sales would not be taken into account when calculating the business turnover (to see if the VAT threshold had been reached). When such a business registered for VAT, it could only claim back a certain proportion of the VAT it had paid on purchases made. Your accountant or VAT office could advise further on this.

Penalties for late or non-registration for VAT are severe. A business in which the turnover has exceeded the threshold may well have to pay the appropriate VAT even though the clients have not been charged at VAT-inclusive rates. This is one of the reasons why good financial forecasting systems are required – if your systems are accurate, you will know when you are likely to be approaching the VAT registration threshold and can register and charge accordingly.

ITQ 25 List the set-up costs you might need to cover when starting a business:

ITQ 26 List the costs you would incur once employing staff:

ITQ 27 List the costs associated with your premises that you would incur once the business was established:

ITQ 28 Under what circumstances would a business have to register for VAT?

ITQ 29 When might it be advantageous to the business to register for VAT, even if it didn't have to?

CATEGORIES OF VAT

Whether, and at what rate, VAT is payable on an item or service purchased will depend on how the item is categorized by HM Revenue and Customs.

1. **Exempt items.** Items may be **exempt** from VAT – i.e. they fall outside the scope of VAT. VAT-exempt items and services currently include land, insurance, postal services and finance. You will not therefore be charged VAT on your bank charges or insurance premiums for example and could not charge VAT on postal costs if you were to run a mail order business.

   Unless items are specifically listed as exempt in the VAT legislation, they are subject to VAT. If in doubt, check with your accountant or the VAT Office (libraries also often have copies of legislative documents and reference books).

2. **Zero-rated items.** The second category of goods and services are those that are **zero-rated**. This means that the items are subject to VAT but that the rate to be charged is currently 0%. Items which are zero-rated include food, animal (but not pet) feed, books, children's clothes, water and sewerage charges, transport and drugs and medicines. The legislation covering what falls into each category is very specific. For instance, riding hats up to size 6¾ in (jockey skulls size 1) are categorized as children's clothing, and thus zero-rated, but this does not apply to larger, adult sizes. If in doubt, it is safest to check with your local HM Revenue and Customs office, or look on their website www.hmrc.gov.uk.

3. **Standard-rated items.** This category of goods and services includes those on which VAT is chargeable at the **standard rate**. This, at the time of publication, means that VAT is chargeable at 17.5%.

4. **Reduced rated items.** A reduced rate of VAT (currently 5%) is applicable to domestic fuel and power only – e.g. electricity, gas, heating oil and coal purchased by businesses or the householder.

CHARGING VAT

If VAT is payable on the item or services being supplied, whether or not it is charged will depend on the status of the business selling the goods or services.

   VAT can only be charged by businesses that are registered for VAT with HM Revenue and Customs. This will mean that although a particular item may fall within the realms of standard rate VAT (e.g. bedding), your supplier will not charge it if their business is not VAT-registered. Likewise, if you are not registered for VAT, you may not charge it on your sales.

ITQ 30 When would a business not be able to register for VAT with HM Revenue and Customs?

ITQ 31 When might HM Revenue and Customs consider exempting a business from VAT registration?

ITQ 32 What does 'VAT-exempt' mean?

ITQ 33 Give an example of a VAT-exempt service or item.

ITQ 34 Explain the term 'zero-rated'.

ITQ 35 Give an example of a service or item that is zero-rated.

ITQ 36 To what does the reduced rate of VAT apply?

PREPARING A CASH FLOW FORECAST

Usually summarized monthly, the cash flow forecast shows the amount of money expected to be paid into the business against the expected expenses in the same period and thus predicts the expected balance of cash available (or not, in most cases!). It is the forecast of cash flowing in and out of the business account. Credit sales and purchases will be shown in the month in which payment is received or made, not in the month that the sale or purchase is made.

There are at least two possible methods of preparing a cash flow forecast:

1. Work out competitive fees (i.e. fees comparable to those charged by other businesses in your area) and from these calculate your forecast sales revenue. Then calculate the costs you will incur to make such a level of sales. Finally, check that the sales revenue is sufficient to cover costs and if not, adjust the fees or look at limiting the costs accordingly.

2. Start by working out your costs. Then calculate the sales revenue you will need to make to cover the costs and work out the fees you will need to charge to achieve the forecast sales revenue. If the required fees are not competitive, i.e. they work out very expensive, look at reducing costs or increasing the number of sales.

Either method is valid. The following example uses the first method. Note that, in the first year of business, it is unlikely that our example livery business will reach the VAT threshold so it will not need to be registered for VAT. Therefore the sales figures in the cash flow forecast do not include VAT. Purchase figures *do* include VAT but these amounts cannot be reclaimed as the business is not VAT-registered.

If and when the turnover reaches the threshold for VAT, the business would be registered and VAT would be shown in separate rows in the cash flow forecast.

Each row in the example cash flow has been given an identification letter for the purpose of explanation. You do not need to do this when planning your own cash flow.

THE CASH FLOW FORECAST EXPLAINED

The rows below refer to those in Table 1, page 36.

The Starting Balance

This is shown in row A. In Month 1 this business starts with nothing in the bank. Thereafter, the closing balance of one month becomes the starting balance of the next.

Receipts (Inflow) – Expected Sales Revenue

This category has row B as its overall heading and runs on to row G.

For a new business, the expected sales revenue would be based entirely on *assumptions*. Care must be taken to ensure that assumptions are realistic and achievable. In order to calculate the expected sales revenue, you will need to work out the fees to be charged for each sales category. The following should be considered when making your initial calculation of fees to be charged:

- What is the minimum you need to charge in order to cover your costs?
- What would seem to be a reasonable fee for the service?
- What do your competitors charge?

Fees charged for services will vary slightly between businesses. Once a business is well established and has developed an excellent reputation fees are often increased to reflect this. You will need to develop a sales plan or schedule for all categories of sales.

Our example cash flow forecast (Table 1) makes the following assumptions regarding fees to be charged:

1. Lessons   1 hour   £ 10.00 each
2. Liveries   Full   £ 300.00 per calendar month

These fees exclude VAT.

Your business may have other categories of sales. We have kept to two only for simplicity.

ROW C – LESSONS

Initially there will be four school horses who can be used for lessons. The owner has decided that each horse should work a maximum of two hours per day and that each should have two days off per week if possible.

4 horses x 2 hours per day = 8 teaching hours per day.

8 hours x 5 days per week = 40 teaching hours per week.

40 teaching hours @ £10 per hour = £ 400 per week potential income through teaching on school horses.

£400 x 52 ÷ 12 = £1,733.33 per calendar month (pcm).

- For the purposes of cash flow, always round figures up or down to the nearest fifty or hundred, and never mention pennies!

Therefore, for the purposes of our cash flow, the maximum monthly income through lessons (if school horse numbers remain the same) is £1,750.

Take into account that you will not start off with the maximum number of teaching hours. This will take time to build up. These hours may be split between group lessons of varying sizes (obviously up to a maximum of four riders per lesson). This split is not important for the purposes of the cash flow forecast.

Even if the business could attract sufficient clients for the horses to be fully utilized, there may be other factors that would have to be taken into account when the business's earnings for lessons were forecast. These may include:

- The number of instructors available.

- The number of arenas available – even if three instructors were available to hold separate lessons, this could not happen if there was insufficient space available for three lessons to be run at the same time.

- The effects of the weather – is an indoor school or all-weather surface available?

- Allowances for staff sickness and non-availability of horses through illness or injury.

- The other major factor to be considered is the number of clients who might be expected to use the facilities. A riding school within easy reach of major population centres might be expected to have a bigger client base than one set up in a remote, rural area. The remote business may, however, have a more captive audience in that there may be fewer businesses in the area competing for the available clients. All of these factors should be investigated and considered when calculating forecast sales.

For the purposes of planning the cash flow, the extent to which the teaching builds up can be calculated on a percentage basis:

Months 1 and 2	10% =	£175 pcm
Month 3	20% =	£350 pcm
Months 4 and 5	40% =	£700 pcm
Months 6 and 7	50% =	£875 pcm
Month 8	60% =	£1,050 pcm
Month 9	70% =	£1,225 pcm
Months 10 and 11	80% =	£1,400 pcm
Month 12	100% =	£1,750 pcm

- These figures will not be an exact representation of sales. Obviously it is impossible to predict *exactly* what will happen in the future. The percentages used are based on common-sense assumptions.

- In the cash flow these figures will be rounded up or down to the nearest fifty or hundred. This will not have a detrimental impact on the forecast as the actual figures will not be identical anyway.

ROW D – LIVERIES

We will assume there are no liveries in Month 1, but the business builds up to four liveries by Month 6.

Month 1 – 0 liveries	=	nil pcm
Month 2 – 1 livery	=	£300 pcm
Month 3 – 2 liveries	=	£600 pcm

Month 4 – 2 liveries   =   £600 pcm
Month 5 – 3 liveries   =   £900 pcm
Month 6 – 4 liveries   =   £1,200 pcm

Assume this is to stay the same until Month 12, when the business loses a livery.

ROW E – CAPITAL INTRODUCED
This is usually the amount of cash you are able to allocate from your own resources. In our example the owner has invested £1,000 in Month 1.

ROW F – BANK LOAN
This is the amount we think we are going to need. Having completed the cash flow it may become clear that we need to borrow more. The bank may or may not lend more – they may suggest taking an overdraft instead of a larger loan (see later this chapter).

ROW G – TOTAL RECEIPTS
Rows C to F added together.

Payments (Outflow) – Expected Costs
This category has row H as its overall heading and is further divided into:

- **Direct costs** – rows I, J, K
- **Indirect costs** – rows L–T

With row U giving the overall total costs.

For simplicity we have not included too many categories. You can probably think of further payment categories. You could (but do not *need* to) divide the costs into 'direct costs' and 'overheads' or 'indirect costs'.

Later on, however, it will be necessary to prepare a forecast profit and loss budget and for this the payments *do* need to be divided into direct costs and overheads. Therefore, if we split the figures now in the cash flow, it will help later on.

ROW I – WAGES
These can be calculated according to the expected level of sales – how many staff will be needed to support the expected sales? Don't forget to allow for PAYE and National Insurance contributions when calculating your wages bill.

In our example the business will not support (or need) staff in the first 4 months. The owner of the business is likely to try to manage without help. As the business develops and starts to earn money, so part-time staff can be taken on to help. This can be built up to a full-time member of staff later on in the first year.

Our example business is run by an individual operating as a sole trader. The business owner *does not* take wages. The business owner takes **drawings.** These are dealt with differently from wages in terms of accounting and deductions. This will be explained fully further on.

ROW J – FEED, HAY AND BEDDING

The expected cost of feed, hay and bedding needs to take into account the number of horses on the yard, the type of work they are doing and the time of year. Also consider whether hay and straw will be purchased in bulk when it is harvested or in smaller batches throughout the year.

ROW K – FARRIER AND VET

The expected cost of shoeing and preventative veterinary and worming treatment can be calculated based on the number of school horses in the yard. Other routine and emergency veterinary treatment will also need to be allowed for – although this is a bit more difficult. It would be unrealistic to assume that the vet would not have to be called out at all during the year and a judgement as to the level of veterinary care that might realistically be required needs to be made in the form of an 'educated guess'.

Alternatively, you may insure the horses against vets' bills – if so, allowance for this should be included within the insurance estimate. Don't forget to allow for any 'excess' payments (the first £100 or so of the claim value, normally paid by the claimant).

Your cash flow does not need to include the veterinary and farriery costs of the livery horses as these should be invoiced direct to the horses' owners.

Indirect Costs
ROW L – MOTOR EXPENSES

This may include a 'pool car' and the horsebox. Allow for the costs of maintaining and running the vehicle(s).

ROW M – ADVERTISING

It is essential to advertise the business in order to attract customers. This example business has a modest advertising allowance but could look to increase this in time.

ROW N – RENT AND UTILITIES

The cost of renting premises is usually a fixed amount per month and can be easily forecast. You may be required to pay business rates – advice on this should be sought from the local authority. An allowance for water rates should be included.

In our example, we assume there will be a 10-year lease on premises providing 10 stables, tack and feed rooms, hay barn, office, an outdoor school and 10 acres of grazing. The monthly rent is £800 which includes the business and water rates.

Note that you must seek the advice of your solicitor before signing a lease. Allow for the cost of such advice in your set-up costs. Also note that you may have to pay **stamp duty** to HM Revenue and Customs, based on the value of the lease.

ROW O – INSURANCE

An allowance should be made for all types of insurance needed to meet both statutory and business requirements. This may include Public Liability, Employers' Liability, Buildings and Contents Insurance, insurance on the horses in the yard and insurance on the business proprietor. Seek quotations from insurance brokers and companies. Insurance premiums can be paid monthly by direct debit.

ROW P – OFFICE AND PHONE

The expected telephone costs and costs for electricity and other fuels such as heating oil should be included here. An allowance also needs to be made for the costs of stationery and office consumables for equipment such as toner and ink cartridges for printers, and for postage and printing.

ROW Q – BANK CHARGES

The bank will usually charge businesses quarterly in arrears based on the number of transactions in the period concerned, although they may allow a new business a period of free banking. We have made a monthly allowance for these charges. Loan repayments are usually paid monthly. In the first year of trading approximately £300 will be paid in interest and bank charges, and £800 will be paid off the loan.

ROW R – REPAIRS AND RENEWALS

These figures allow for some ongoing repairs.

ROW S – CAPITAL EXPENDITURE/LEASEHOLD IMPROVEMENTS

The business will need to make purchases of capital equipment during the year. The example forecast includes the elements of capital expenditure detailed under set-up costs. As many of these costs are associated with improvements to the premises they are often called 'leasehold improvements'.

The following costs are included in Row S of Table 1:

Paddock maintenance equipment	£300
Building and fencing materials	£1,650
Arena improvements	£2,500
Fire safety equipment	£250
Feed bins and office furniture	£250
Miscellaneous yard equipment	£200
Miscellaneous tack and rugs	£800
	£5,950

The set-up costs have been spread over the first year as you are unlikely to rush out in the first month and incur all of these costs. Most suppliers will allow you to open a trade account, allowing you to be invoiced for the items on 30 days credit.

ROW T – DRAWINGS

In our example the owner has taken only modest drawings, allowing for the fact that it takes time to build up the business. As the business develops, so drawings can increase. Once the business is well established and the sales have increased, the owner could expect to (and would need to) take more drawings from the business.

ROW U – TOTAL PAYMENTS
The total of all cash flowing out.

Net Cash Flow and Closing Balance
ROW V – NET FLOW IN OR (OUT)
This row shows the difference between Row G (total receipts) and Row U (total payments). It shows how much cash has flowed in or out of the business. Negatives are shown in brackets.

ROW W – CLOSING BALANCE
This row shows the difference between Row A (starting balance) and Row V (net flow in or out). It shows the business's anticipated financial position. As mentioned earlier, the closing balance of one month becomes the starting balance of the next.

At the end of the first year it seems that our business is in a negative position of minus £6,000.

You would therefore need to consider the following:

1. How can you increase the sales figures?

2. Should you charge more for lessons or liveries to increase cash flowing in?

3. Should you consider spending more on advertising to increase sales levels?

4. Do you need more school horses to allow more lessons to be given?

5. Can you reduce your outgoings anywhere?

6. Capital expenditure is a one-off cost to the business until that item wears out. In Year 2 of trading, will your capital expenditure be reduced?

If the above considerations cannot be implemented for any reason you are definitely going to need further financial help. This could be in the form of an overdraft of at least £6,000, or a larger loan.

PREPARING A PROFIT AND LOSS FORECAST

A profit and loss forecast (or account) shows anticipated gross and net profit over an epoch of time, normally one year, and is based on the figures from the cash flow forecast for the period concerned.

A VAT-registered business would exclude VAT from the figures in the profit and loss forecast as it would claim back all VAT on payments and pass all VAT collected on sales to HM Revenue and Customs. For a business not

		Month 1	Month 2	Month 3	Month 4	Month 5	Month 6	Month 7	Month 8	Month 9	Month 10	Month 11	Month 12	Total
A	**Starting balance**	Nil	4,650	3,700	1650	1200	450	(1700)	(2450)	(3450)	(3900)	(4350)	(5000)	
B	**RECEIPTS (Inflow)**													
C	Lessons	150	200	350	700	700	850	850	1050	1200	1400	1400	1650	10 500
D	Liveries		300	600	600	900	1200	1200	1200	1200	1200	1200	900	10 500
E	Capital introduced	1000												1000
F	Bank loan	5000												5000
G	**TOTAL RECEIPTS**	6150	500	950	1300	1600	2050	2050	2250	2400	2600	2600	2550	27 000
H	**PAYMENTS (Outflow)**													
	Direct costs													
I	Wages					400	600	600	800	800	800	800	800	5600
J	Feed, hay, bedding	100	150	200	200	250	300	300	300	300	400	400	400	3300
K	Farrier/vet		100		100		150		100		150		100	700
	Indirect costs													
L	Motor expenses	50	50	50	50	50	50	50	50	50	50	50	200	750
M	Advertising			100			100			100			100	400
N	Rent/utilities	800	800	800	800	800	800	800	800	800	800	800	800	9600
O	Insurance	50	50	50	50	50	50	50	50	50	50	50	50	600
P	Office/phone			250			250			250			250	1000
Q	Bank charges (inc. loan repayment)		100	100	100	100	100	100	100	100	100	100	100	1100
R	Repairs and renewals					200			200			200		600
S	Capital expenditure/ leasehold improvements	500		1250	250	300	1600	500	450		300	450	350	5950
T	Drawings		200	200	200	200	200	400	400	400	400	400	400	3400
U	**TOTAL PAYMENTS**	1500	1450	3000	1750	2350	4200	2800	3250	2850	3050	3250	3550	33 000
V	**NET FLOW IN (OUT) (G – U)**	4650	(950)	(2050)	(450)	(750)	(2150)	(750)	(1000)	(450)	(450)	(650)	(1000)	(6000)
W	**CLOSING BALANCE (A – V)**	4650	3700	1650	1200	450	(1700)	(2450)	(3450)	(3900)	(4350)	(5000)	(6000)	

Table 1 An example cash flow forcast

registered for VAT, VAT on payments is included in the profit and loss forecast – the company cannot claim the VAT back and it is therefore a legitimate expense.

Table 2 shows an example profit and loss forecast based on the figures included in the cash flow forecast at Table 1.

Rows in cash		Amount (£)
flow C and D	Sales (net of VAT)	21 000
I,J and K	Less: direct costs	9600
	Gross profit	**11 400**
	Overheads	
L	Motor expenses	750
M	Advertising	400
N	Rent and utilities	9600
O	Insurance	600
P	Office and phone	1000
Q	Interest charges	300
R	Repairs and renewals	600
	Total overheads	**13 250**
	Trading profit (loss)	**(1850)**
	Less depreciation	1390
	Net profit (loss) before tax	**£ (3240)**

Table 2 An example profit and loss forecast

When preparing the profit and loss forecast, the following points should be noted:

1. Credit sales must be entered when they are made, *not* when the cash is collected – this can be one or two months later.

2. Similarly, expenses must be entered when they are incurred, *not* when they are paid.

3. Costs should be broken down between direct and indirect costs.

4. Do not include capital items, bank loan or assets purchased.

5. Depreciation on the assets must be calculated and included.

ITQ 37 Summarize two possible methods of preparing a cash flow forecast.

1.

2.

ITQ 38 What might a new business consider when calculating fees to be charged?

RAISING INITIAL FINANCE

Once the business plan, cash flow forecast and profit and loss forecast have been completed you can answer the following questions:

- Do I need to borrow money?
- If so, how much?
- When?
- How am I going to pay it back?
- What security can I offer?
- How much can I afford to repay each month?
- Are any grants available?

In our example, it would appear from the cash flow forecast that the business needs to borrow approximately £11,000 to cover the initial investment it needs to make in capital assets. This is likely to comprise part bank loan, part overdraft.

When seeking a bank loan or overdraft it is essential that expert advice is sought from the bank manager, accountant or small business adviser. Armed with the answers to the above questions, get quotes from different reliable sources and find out:

- What is the cost of borrowing money?
- When and how will the cost be paid?
- Over what period will the repayments be made?
- What will be the total expenditure?
- What extra charges might be involved?

BANK LOAN

Your bank manager will advise on the best terms and conditions for a business loan. Loans are taken out over a set period and are usually repaid in monthly instalments. Some form of security is normally needed and additional life assurance/insurance will need to be taken out. There are often charges associated with setting up a loan, depending on the individual bank's policy.

OVERDRAFT FACILITY

Often the simplest form of finance a business can use is an **overdraft** – an extension of credit on the business's current account. The bank may agree to set a pre-arranged limit on the overdraft amount and this limit is reviewed periodically. The bank will insist that the overdraft is repayable on demand but this does not usually happen, provided you are seen to be running the business as planned and do not exceed the limit. The bank will need to see cash flow and profit and loss forecasts before agreeing the overdraft.

The bank is likely to charge an **annual fee** for the facility and interest on the actual amount of the overdraft. The interest paid on an overdraft would usually be the same as for a business loan.

SMALL FIRMS LOAN GUARANTEE SCHEME

This is a Government-sponsored scheme designed to assist small businesses unable to borrow from the bank because of a lack of security. The scheme is administered by the Department of Business, Enterprise and Regulatory Reform (BERR).

In return for a premium paid by the business, the Government will guarantee up to 70% of a loan up to £100,000 for a new business as long as the bank would have lent the money if security had been available. Many banks operate this scheme and some can lend up to £30,000 without prior BERR approval.

CHAPTER SUMMARY

There is a lot of work to do before taking the decision to start your own business. It is best practice to take the time to prepare properly, looking into all the possible pitfalls before taking the plunge and perhaps opening yourself up to potentially large financial losses. Family members also need to be aware of the degree of support you might need from them. They will need to consider whether they will be prepared to accept you working long hours for, initially at least, a meagre income.

This chapter has introduced the main principles of planning a business. Try to seek as much advice as possible from experienced business people and professionals such as business advisers and accountants. There are business consultants available but very often their services are expensive. Local organizations such as 'Business Link' offer free advice to prospective business owners.

Select a few good books on the subject of running a business – there is a huge range available.

Having looked at what is involved in the planning stage, we now go on to explain what you need to do next, having decided to go ahead and start your business.

CHAPTER 2

FINANCIAL MANAGEMENT

The aims and objectives of this chapter are to explain:

- Why financial records are kept.
- Which records need to be kept.
- How to record everyday transactions.
- How to complete banking paperwork.
- How to check the bank statement.
- The importance of updating the cash flow.

From day one of managing either a new or existing business, you will need to handle everyday financial transactions. You need to develop effective systems for recording financial transactions that can be maintained easily.

As with the information in Chapter 1, that provided within this chapter is intended as a guide and should be used in conjunction with professional advice from your accountant.

The examples of systems and procedures included represent a financial management system that could be used or adapted for use taking into account the professional advice you receive.

RECORD-KEEPING

We start by looking at the methods of record-keeping. There are numerous books written on the subjects of book-keeping and financial management. Whilst it is beyond the scope of this book to discuss these specialist subjects fully, there are certain matters any equestrian business manager needs to understand in principle.

THE NEED TO KEEP RECORDS

Records must be kept both to satisfy legal (or statutory) requirements (i.e. these are mandatory) and for management purposes

The records kept because of legal requirements may also be helpful for management purposes. There is a statutory requirement to keep adequate records of receipts and payments so that HM Revenue and Customs can assess your profits for tax purposes. If a business is registered for VAT, HM

Revenue and Customs may carry out an inspection and would require access to records of receipts and payments.

Good financial records will also help you to answer the following questions:

- What are the variable costs?
- What are the overheads?
- What profit is the business making?
- Is it necessary to register for VAT?
- What is the value of fixed and current assets?
- How much does the business owe?
- How much is owed to the business?
- What is the current cash position of the business?

Therefore effective day-to-day financial management ensures that:

- The overall performance of the business is constantly and closely monitored.

- Cash flow is managed effectively.

- Problems can be spotted in advance and action taken.

At the end of the financial year your accountant will use your records to produce the business's **annual accounts** (also called **annual financial statements**). These are submitted to HM Customs and Revenue who use them to assess:

- For sole traders and partnerships, the amount of income tax and National Insurance Contributions (NICs) payable.

- For companies, the amount of corporation tax payable.

Company accounts for a limited company may also have to be audited by an independent accountant if the turnover reaches the designated threshold. A copy of a limited company's accounts is sent to Companies House who use them to check that the company is not trading insolvently. Anyone can contact Companies House and ask to see the accounts of a limited company so a degree of privacy is lost.

RECORDS WHICH SHOULD BE KEPT

The records kept depend to a certain extent upon the nature of the business, but the main requirements include:

'Dawn of day one' records These are the figures recorded on day one of the business's first financial year. Your accountant will call these your **opening balances**.

Cash records	Records of daily receipts and payments made by cash or cheque must be kept in order to calculate profit and loss. A petty cash book should be kept for small, low value purchases.
Bank account records	All banking transactions must be checked by preparing bank reconciliation statements regularly.
VAT records	If the business is VAT-registered with HM Revenue and Customs, VAT records must be kept.
Wages records	These must be kept when staff are employed.

PREPARING FOR THE START OF BUSINESS

Before you start trading:

1. Decide which book-keeping system to use – our examples are based on a simple analysed cash book which can be adapted for use on a computer system.

2. Have a filing system ready for the efficient storage of invoices (explained later in this chapter).

3. If you have started a business in a self-employed capacity, notify HM Revenue and Customs and the National Insurance Contributions Office. If you have formed a company, your solicitor will advise on the steps to be taken.

4. If your turnover is forecast to be more than the VAT registration threshold you will need to notify HM Revenue and Customs and register for VAT.

Full information is available on HM Revenue and Customs' website: www.hmrc.gov.uk.

ITQ 39 Give the two main reasons why a business should keep financial records:

1.

2.

ITQ 40 Give three reasons why a business needs to have an effective financial management system:

1.

2.

3.

ITQ 41 What tax liabilities might your annual accounts be used to calculate?

Computerized Systems

It is well worth using a computerized system for your record-keeping. Discuss with your accountant the best system to use – ideally your system should be compatible with the system used by your accountant. This will help when your accountant is preparing your annual accounts, thereby saving the accountant time and you money. When preparing the columns for analysis, consult your accountant so that these are in line with the way in which he or she prepares your accounts.

There is a wide range of systems available, the best known and most widely used of which include QuickBooks, Sage and Microsoft Money. The packages vary in complexity and should ideally include an integrated payroll. Every time a transaction is entered onto the system it is accounted for, with the totals changing accordingly. The system does all the necessary calculations.

THE START OF BUSINESS

Records must to be maintained from the first moment of the first day of business, i.e. 'dawn of day one'. An opening balance sheet must be drawn up showing all assets and liabilities.

The Balance Sheet

This demonstrates the value of the business at a particular point of time. It shows the value of assets held by the business against the capital introduced by the business's owner and liabilities owed to third parties.

For example – assume our new business owner introduces horses worth £3,000, tack and equipment worth £2,950 and £1,000 cash. The cash flow forecast identified a need for additional finance so a loan of £5,000 has been taken out which will be used to pay for improvements to the establishment. Table 3 demonstrates how this situation can be represented in a balance sheet.

	£	£	
Fixed assets			
Horses	3,000		
Tack/equipment	2,950	5,950	**(1)**
Current assets			
Cash at bank		6,000	**(2)**
less			
Current liabilities	–	–	**(3)**
Net current assets		6,000	**(4) = (2) – (3)**
Long-term liabilities			
Bank loan		5,000	**(5)**
Net assets		£6,950	**(6) = (1) + (4) – (5)**
Financed by			
Capital introduced		£6,950	
Capital employed		£6,950	

Table 3 An example opening balance sheet

Note: If sum 4 is positive then it is included in net current assets. If negative then it is included in net current liabilities.

The balance sheet shows that the business currently has assets to the value of £6,950 and that the source of these assets was the proprietor. In other words, the proprietor has introduced capital of £6,950.

How the balance sheet changes with trading will be covered later in this chapter.

ITQ 42 What is checked by Companies House when the required copy of a limited company's accounts is sent to them?

ITQ 43 What does an opening balance sheet show?

RECORDING RECEIPTS

Receipts can be recorded in the following places:

1. **Business bookings diary** – this tends to be the business's daily working diary which includes details of all bookings and engagements. It is always normally to hand in the office so is often the first place that payment details are recorded.

2. **Daily receipts diary** – this is kept solely for recording daily receipts (normally done at the end of the working day) prior to transferring details to either the:

3. **Cash book**

    or:

4. **Computer system**

- *Note that the cash book can form part of a computer system so, from hereon, 'cash book' will refer to either a manual analysed cash book or a computer system. Computer systems are easier, quicker and more interesting to use than a manual system.*

DAILY RECEIPTS

The **daily receipts diary** is used to record individual receipts (or **takings**) at the end of each day and can be used to update the cash book. If running the sort of business in which customers are booked in for daily lessons or livery owners are incurring additional costs, you will need to keep a **business bookings diary** as well as the daily receipts diary.

In the bookings diary you will have a record of things such as clients booked for lessons, hiring of the arena, clipping of livery horses, etc. When a client makes a cash or cheque payment for such an item write the amount and method of payment against the relevant entry in the bookings diary. Also enter details of the receipt into the daily receipts diary.

The daily receipts diary and cash book should only include cash or cheque actually received on that day.

If a credit client has booked a service, e.g. a livery client has a lesson booked, write the amount owed and 'Acc' or similar against the client's name in the business diary. The credit sale should then be entered into the client's **account record** (see Table 4) and invoiced periodically as agreed. Payment for the invoiced amount will only be entered in the daily receipts diary and cash book once it is actually received.

A credit client's account record can be kept on a card index system or within a book or ring binder. A computer record could be kept, although in a busy yard it tends to be easier to jot things down in the bookings diary or onto the client's account record rather than turn on the computer and enter the details. Obviously a large yard would employ a full-time secretary who could keep computer records up to date.

The computer record or written record would form the basis of the client's monthly invoice.

CLIENT ACCOUNT RECORD

Paula Jones Holly Cottage Park View Road Melchett Suffolk IP59 2PW		January 2010
Date	**Details**	**Amount Payable £**
1/1/10	Livery to 31 Jan 2010	300.00
5/1/10	Hire indoor school	10.00
7/1/10	Lesson	10.00
10/1/10	Hire indoor school	10.00
21/1/10	Lesson	10.00
31/1/10	Lesson	10.00
	TOTAL	350.00
	Invoice Number	99001
	Invoice Date	31 January 2010

Table 4 An example client account record

ITQ 44 When preparing to start a business, which Government departments might you have to notify?

ITQ 45 List two other things you will need to do before starting to trade:

1.

2.

ITQ 46 What is the purpose of the daily receipts diary?

Table 5 shows how cash or cheque payments could be entered into the daily receipts diary. The business in the example is not registered for VAT so a VAT column is not included and no VAT is shown in the VAT row.

Date: 3 February 2010						
Name	**Details**	**Type cash/chq**	**Cash clients**	**Credit clients**		
			Amount	Inv. no	Amount	
S. Smith	Group lesson	Cash	10.00			
Mrs Jones	January account	Chq		99001	350.00	
J. Jones	Group lesson	Cash	10.00			
A. Wright	Group lesson	Chq	10.00			
Sarah Hunt	Clinic on 4/2	Chq	35.00			
Julie Jarvis	Group lesson	Cash	10.00			
						TOTALS
	Total		75.00		350.00	425.00
	VAT					
	Net total		75.00		350.00	
	Total Receipts		**75.00**		**350.00**	**425.00**
	Cash					30.00
	Cheques					395.00

Table 5 An example page of a daily receipts diary

THE CASH BOOK – RECEIPTS

Left-hand pages in the cash book should be used for recording all receipts. The pages on the right are used to record payments (as explained later in this chapter). Where a computer system is used, the receipts will be entered onto the relevant spreadsheet.

Each page or spreadsheet of the cash book is divided into columns. Column headings should reflect the categories of receipts you wish to use to monitor the financial status of your business. These columns are known as **analysis columns**.

You will have given the column headings some thought when preparing your cash flow forecast as part of your business plan, as explained in Chapter 1. You should also have sought the advice of your accountant at the planning stage. Consider also the number of columns that will be easily managed – off-the-shelf printed cash books (available from stationers) will have a limited number of columns on each side.

In the example of Table 6, receipts are entered under the headings of livery, lessons, and other. These are the categories of receipts by which the owner has decided to monitor the business.

Date	Details	A Bank	B Cheques	C Cash	D VAT	E Livery	F Lessons	G Other Amount	G Other Details
3.2.10	Daily receipts diary (See Table 5)		395.00	30.00		300.00	105.00	20.00	Hire indoor school
4.2.10	Banked	425.00							
6.2.10	Daily receipts diary		100.00	50.00			110.00	40.00	Clipping
7.2.10	Daily receipts diary		300.00	80.00		300.00	80.00		
7.2.10	To petty cash	50.00							
7.2.10	Banked	480.00							
28.2.10	Daily receipts diary		20.00	60.00			80.00		
28.2.10	Banked	80.00							
	TOTAL	1035.00	815.00	220.00		600.00	375.00	60.00	

Table 6 An example page from a cash book – receipts

A = B + C = D + E + F + G

Column A The total banked. The figures in this column should match your paying-in book slips (minus any amount put into petty cash). The total figure is reached by adding together rows B and C. Note that sales from 6.2.10 and 7.2.10 amounted to £530. £50 of this was put into petty cash and £480 was banked.

Column B All cheques received.

Column C All cash received.

Column D As this business is not VAT-registered, VAT is not shown separately. Later on we discuss record-keeping if VAT-registered.

Column E Livery payments. Of the £425 received on 3 February, £300 was made up of livery fees. See Table 4 – P Jones has incurred a £300 fee which became due when invoice 99001 was sent.

Column F Lesson payments. Of the £425 received on 3 February, £105.00 was made up of lessons.

Column G Other receipts. Of the £425 received on 3 February, £20 was for hire of the indoor school. See Table 4 – P Jones hired the indoor school twice in January.

The amounts for livery and lessons can be identified from the bookings diary, client account records and daily receipts diary. It will be easier to track receipts from bank statements and paying-in slips later if total amounts paid by cheque and cash are given.

If registered for VAT, you will need to identify the amount of VAT attributable to the receipts entered in the cash book. The individual receipts shown under the category headings will be net (exclusive) of VAT.

As each page of the cash book is used, the totals in each column should be calculated and taken forward to the following pages until the end of the month, when the columns should be ruled off and totals calculated. A computerized system does this automatically.

ITQ 47 What should you consider when deciding on column headings for the receipts side of your cash book?

END OF DAY PROCEDURE

At the end of each day:

1. Transfer details of any credit sales, identified in the business bookings diary, onto the client's account record so that they can be invoiced at the end of the period concerned.

2. Update the receipts (or sales) side of the cash book using the entries in the daily receipts diary.

3. Enter any other receipts that are not written in the daily receipts diary into the cash book receipts side.

4. Enter any receipts that do not fall into categories covered by your column headings into a column headed 'other' – give a short explanation in the details column.

5. Empty the till or cash box and count the contents – ensure that the total tallies with the record of receipts, if not, resolve any differences. The normal float, used for giving change, can then be returned to the cash box (see The Petty Cash Book, later this chapter).

Updating the cash book on a daily basis will:

● Help you to keep a better track of the business's financial position.

● Allow any errors or anomalies, like the possibility of fraud occurring between records to be quickly resolved.

● Take less time than updating on a weekly or monthly basis as all events are fresh in your mind and records are easily to hand.

SALES INVOICES

As well as recording cash or cheque takings you will need to prepare sales invoices for customers for whom you have opened an account. The invoice will cover all goods and services received by the client in the period concerned. Table 7 shows the invoice raised to cover the client account record at Table 4. Note that the VAT column is blank as the business is not registered for VAT.

ITQ 48 Against what date should cash and cheque receipts be written in the cash book?

ITQ 49 Summarize the end of day procedure for updating records of your receipts.

THE EQUESTRIAN CENTRE INVOICE			

Invoice to: Paula Jones Holly Cottage Park View Road Melchett Suffolk IP59 2PW	Invoice number Invoice date Payable by	99001 31 Jan 2010 7 Feb 2010

Date	Details	Net £	VAT £	Gross £
	ACCOUNT FOR JAN 2010			
Jan 08	**Livery** – 1 month to 31 January 2010	300.00		300.00
	Lessons 7/1, 21/1, 31/1 at £10 each	30.00		30.00
	Hire charges			
5/1	Indoor school	10.00		10.00
10/1	Indoor school	10.00		10.00
	TOTAL	**350.00**		**350.00**

The Equestrian Centre
Wrabbing Road, Melchett, Suffolk, IP59 2RC

Please make cheques payable to The Equestrian Centre

Table 7 An invoice for a credit account client

The following summarizes a simple procedure that could be followed for account customers:

1. Agree terms on which the account will be operated. For example, an invoice will be rendered for all services at the end of each month, which is payable within 7 days.

2. Keep a record of all invoices raised in a tabular form. This should include columns for:

   ● A sequential invoice number.
   ● The date the invoice was raised.

- Who the invoice was raised upon.
- The amount of the invoice.
- The date payment was received.

This will help you to refer back to invoices later in your financial year if necessary and provides a quick and easy way of checking which invoices are outstanding.

3. Prepare all invoices promptly (very important if invoices are payable on a short timescale) and include all details of charges, together with the date on which payment is due.

4. Keep a copy in a file for 'unpaid invoices'. If the invoice is for a livery client it is a good idea to keep a copy in the client's livery file.

5. When the cheque is received, take the invoice out of the unpaid file and write on it the date on which payment was received together with the cheque number. Also write these details on your invoice record sheet.

6. Record the receipt in the daily receipts diary.

7. Pay the amount received into the bank, together with any other cheque or cash takings.

8. Transfer the copy of the invoice into a 'paid invoices' file.

Summarizing the invoice by the categories used in the columns of the cash book will make it easier to update the cash book when payment is received.

> **ITQ 50** Why is it better to update the cash book daily rather than weekly or monthly?

> **ITQ 51** Against what date would a receipt for a credit customer's invoice be entered in the daily receipts diary and the cash book?

CHEQUE RECEIPTS

Whenever possible, ask for the customer's bank card, check the amount on the card that is guaranteed by the bank (usually £50 or £100) and if the amount payable is less than this write the following details on the back of the cheque:

- Bank card number (check which number is the card number – writing the account number on the cheque will not help you).

- Expiry date.

Check also:

- The customer's signature against that on the reverse of the card.

- That the valid from date (if shown) has already passed.

Cheques properly endorsed with these details are guaranteed to be honoured by the bank and cannot be stopped by the drawer. Make sure that you have a record of the client's name and address if they pay by cheque. Cheques can go astray in the course of clearing and if the cheque is not honoured for any reason you will need to refer back to the client.

PAYING INTO THE BANK

It is not safe to keep large sums of money on the premises – and the money is better employed in the bank account keeping the overdraft down or earning interest and ensuring that there are sufficient funds to cover payments made by the business. Takings must therefore be banked promptly.

However, when paying money into the bank, bear in mind that you may be charged by the bank for processing each paying-in slip as well as for processing each cheque paid in. If the amount to be paid in is quite small and the bank balance or cash flow do not dictate that it should be paid in straight away, you will reduce your bank charges by waiting to pay it in when more payments have been received.

If your business generates large amounts of coins, ask the bank for a supply of coin bags to make counting and carrying the money easier.

Completing the Paying-in Slip

Business bank account holders are normally provided with paying-in books containing paying-in slips. There are usually two copies of each slip, the top copy, usually the bank's copy, is perforated so can be removed easily from the book. Carbon paper is used to make a copy of each slip, which remains in the book.

The reverse of the paying-in slip is usually printed so that you can record details of each cheque that is being paid in. The total number of cheques and amount of cash being paid in is recorded on the front of the slip. If you have a reference or invoice number for cheque receipts, write this underneath the cheque name – this will help later if you need to refer back to the receipt.

Be sure to use the carbon paper so that you have a copy of the slip. When cash and cheques are paid into the bank the total is entered into the 'bank' column of the cash book. This must agree with the paying-in slip and the cheque and cash entries entered, less any cash transferred into petty cash, (see The Petty Cash Book, later this chapter) since the previous time money was paid into the bank.

> **ITQ 52** Having raised an invoice for a credit account client, what will you do with it?

> **ITQ 53** List the details you should check and write on the reverse side of your clients' cheques.

Bank Clearing Systems

It is important to note that, although amounts may be credited to your account on the day that you pay a cheque in, you may not be able to withdraw the money for between 3 and 5 working days (varies by bank and customer status) of paying the cheque in.

If you were to ask your bank for a balance figure on a particular day, they might provide you with two figures, one representing the cleared balance and one representing the statement (or ledger) balance. If you have paid in cheques within a few days of asking for the balance, the cleared balance may be less than the statement balance by the value of the cheques paid in but yet to clear.

- On the day a cheque is paid in, it is forwarded to the head office of the bank at which it was paid in.

- On the second working day it is forwarded to the head office of the bank the cheque was drawn against.

- On the third working day it is forwarded to the account holder's branch and the funds are transferred to your bank branch.

- The account holder's branch, however, has until noon on the fourth working day to send the cheque back in the post unpaid (if not guaranteed with a cheque guarantee card) and notify your branch to return the funds.

- Your branch may therefore not know the 'fate' of the cheque until the fifth working day after you have paid it in.

- So, although the bank may have credited the funds to your account on the first day, you may not be allowed to draw against them until the fifth day.

Internet and PC Banking

Most banks offer on-line PC and internet banking services and if you have a personal computer with a modem or ISDN line connected to it, using this service would almost certainly be to your advantage.

Internet banking allows you to view the status of your account and lists of transactions right up to the minute. As the bank processes a transaction against your account, you will be able to see it, and its effect on your balance, within minutes. You can also authorize certain payments and transactions and set up regular payments from the comfort of your office or home.

Although not usually quite as dynamic as internet banking, since transactions are only usually available up to the end of the last working day, PC banking allows you to work with the information in more ways than internet banking. With PC banking, a connection to the bank's computers is usually made at the start of each session and the transaction record on your computer is updated. Your connection would then be terminated and the information stored on your computer for use. Most PC banking systems will allow you to specify the type of transactions you wish to view, and the period of time you wish to cover. In this way, you could, for instance, print out a bank statement for the preceding month on the very next day, rather than having to wait a week or more for the statement to arrive in the post.

Connections for internet and PC banking systems are encrypted and should only be accessed by whoever has the relevant membership and pass code details. Take advice from the bank regarding the security of your finances over the internet.

ITQ 54 What is the difference between cleared and statement (or ledger) balance?

ITQ 55 Why might your bank not allow you to draw against a cheque deposit for 5 working days?

ITQ 56 What is internet banking?

ITQ 57 Give one difference between internet banking and PC banking:

ITQ 58 Give one advantage of using internet banking compared with traditional banking methods:

PURCHASING

When agreeing to buy (or sell) a service or goods you will be entering into a contract with the supplier (or purchaser). Contract law is a vast subject, beyond the realms of this book. You should, however, understand that both parties will, almost without exception, be entering into a legally binding contract once the following conditions have been met:

1. One party has made an offer to the other – either to buy or to sell.

2. The other party has accepted that offer unconditionally.

3. There is an agreement regarding payment for the goods or services (this may be in form of money or payment in kind – this agreement is known as **consideration**).

4. Both parties have the intention of creating legal relations.

A contract can be made verbally or in writing. A written contract is, however, more readily enforced as it provides proof of what has been agreed.

When making an order for goods or services it is important to make sure that the terms and conditions of the transaction are fully understood by both you and your supplier. As well as being important in terms of enforcing the contract if things go wrong, putting the order in writing will also help to avoid possible misunderstanding of the requirement.

THE PURCHASE ORDER

The main things to include within the order are:

1. What is to be supplied – an exact description of the goods being supplied.

2. The quantity required – is it a one-off service or a finite quantity of goods? Quantities need to be specific – ordering three tons of hay is a lot less open to misinterpretation than ordering a 'lorry load' or 100 bales (weight varies enormously between bales). Weighing the hay on a weighbridge ensures the right quantity is delivered.

3. The quality required or agreed – if there is a specific quality standard required, make sure that this is stated on the order. If you are buying a large quantity of hay, based on the quality of a sample you were provided with, make sure that you keep some of the sample. You can then check that the quality is as promised – you could add 'as sample supplied on…' to your purchase order.

4. Delivery date – when delivery of goods is required, fix realistic, achievable delivery dates that your supplier can meet but that also meet your needs – try to plan ahead so that you avoid buying emergency stocks which could have inflated prices.

5. How will the items be delivered – does the price agreed include delivery by the supplier? If so, who will be responsible for unloading the goods? Make sure the order states what has been agreed in this respect.

6. The price to be paid – agree a price or pricing mechanism before the order is placed.

7. When payment is due – many suppliers will agree to payment being made within 30 or 60 days of delivery – this will help your cash flow.

A purchase order number which is unique to the order should be quoted on the goods delivery note and invoice so the latter documents can be matched to the original purchase order. This will help you prepare the cash flow forecast and income statement.

PAPERWORK FOR PURCHASING

When you have agreed the terms of an order with a supplier and have placed the order, keep a copy of the order in a file for outstanding orders. You could either file these by purchase order number (if you place a lot of orders) or by the agreed delivery date. Filing by the delivery date will help you to summarize the value of outstanding orders due for payment within a particular period. This will be particularly helpful when preparing an up-to-date cash flow forecast for the business.

Keep all other papers related to the order (e.g. supplier's confirmation or acknowledgement) with your file copy of the order.

When the goods are delivered, check that the items have been delivered in accordance with your order, i.e. that the right quantity and right quality have been received. Make sure that you raise any queries promptly. File the supplier's despatch/delivery note with the order and await the supplier's invoice.

When the invoice is received, check it carefully against your copy of the order and, again, raise any queries with the supplier promptly.

ITQ 59 In terms of buying or selling, list the four points which create a legally binding contract:

1.

2.

3.

4.

ITQ 60 List the main things to be included within a written order:

1.

2.

3.

4.

5.

6.

7.

ITQ 61 Why is it better to put an order in writing rather than relying on a verbal agreement?

RECORDING PAYMENTS

We now move on to discuss the method for recording payments made by the business.

When using an analysed cash book, the columns on the right are used for recording payments made to suppliers. When using a computer system a separate spreadsheet is used to enter all payment details. Payments are only recorded when they are actually made, i.e. a cheque has been sent or cash handed over.

Payments for all but small amounts should be made by cheque or credit card rather than by cash. Where cash payments are made, they should be paid and recorded through the petty cash system (see later this chapter).

Several columns are needed in the cash book to analyse the types of payments made (see Table 8). Attention to the number and title of columns used will be time well spent so, as with the sales categories, this should be considered when planning the business. Consult your accountant – if the columns correlate with those used by the accountant it will make his or her job easier at the end of the financial year and will reduce the number of queries and the amount of time spent preparing your accounts. Ultimately, this should save you money.

When deciding which column headings to use, consider which of these will be direct costs and which will be overheads (or indirect costs). Grouping direct and indirect costs together will make it easier to add up and compare with the total direct and indirect costs shown in the end of year accounts. It will help you to understand how the accountant calculates the figures shown on the accounts.

When recording loan repayments, the actual repayment and interest on the loan should be separated. Repayment of the loan amount affects the balance sheet rather than the profit and loss account whereas payments of interest will be included within the profit and loss account.

Since your capital expenditure (for buying fixed assets) will be infrequent, you will only need two columns for them – one for the amount and one to describe the type of asset purchased.

Payments should only be made after the goods or services have been received, against a properly prepared invoice from your supplier. Unpaid invoices should be stored in a file in order of the date upon which they must be paid. If for any reason the invoice has to be stored elsewhere, keep a copy or written description in the file on the appropriate date.

A summary at the front of the file, listing and totalling the invoices to be paid in the current and subsequent months, will help you to keep track of your outstanding liabilities.

MAKING PAYMENTS

Payments should be made at the latest opportunity without exceeding the payment terms detailed on the invoice. Paying the invoice as late as possible within the terms agreed will help your cash flow. However, paying after the due date breaks the terms of your agreement and may affect your supplier's cash flow and consequently make them hesitant about supplying goods or services to you on credit in the future. Late payment may also attract additional charges.

When the payment falls due, write out the cheque, detach the remittance advice slip from the invoice (if one is provided) and send it with the cheque to the creditor. Record the payment in the appropriate column of the cash book.

Remove the copy of the invoice from the unpaid invoice file and update the summary sheet at the front of the file to show that the invoice has been paid. Write on the invoice the date it was paid and the cheque number, and place the copy of the invoice at the front of a file kept for paid invoices.

It will help you later to find the invoice in the file if you allocate a sequential reference number to each invoice paid and file the paid invoices in order of this reference number. Write the number on the invoice and into the cash book against the corresponding payment entry.

If you are paying wages, the amounts paid and all amounts for PAYE and National Insurance should be entered into a wages column.

As with receipts, as each page is used the totals in each column should be calculated and taken forward to the following page until the end of the month, when the columns for payments and receipts should both be ruled off and totals calculated.

If you are registered for VAT you must have a separate column for VAT for both receipts and payments. The figures entered into the analysis columns must then *exclude VAT* (see Chapter 3 VAT Accounting). If, however, you are not registered for VAT then the VAT columns are not necessary and your analysis must be done *including* VAT.

Table 8 demonstrates how the cash book payments side might look.

ITQ 62 How should costs be grouped when planning the column headings in the payments side of the cash book?

ITQ 63 How should loan repayments be recorded?

Known direct debits and standing orders that are paid out of your account should be entered into the payments side of the cash book at the start of each month or against the date on which payment is due to be taken from your account.

If you are VAT-registered, it may be easier to understand the figures, and to avoid making mistakes, if separate columns are used for categories where VAT is not applicable. For instance, there is no VAT on feed or hay but VAT is payable on bedding. Although you might get your feed, hay and bedding from one supplier, and these might appear on the same invoice, showing the cost associated with the items that attract VAT separately will make it easier to understand the VAT figure. We will discuss this further in the next chapter.

Month: February Year: 2010

Direct costs Indirect costs

Date	Details	Ref. Chq No.	Total	VAT	Wages	Feed, hay, bedding	Farrier Vet	Motor exp.	Advert	Rent Utilities	Insurance	Office Phone	Bank charges/ Loan	Drawings	Capital expenditure Amount	Details
2	Hiscock Farms Ltd	01 1514	800.00							800.00						
3	Brown Feeds	02 1515	100.00			100.00										
5	M Black Farrier	03 1516	84.00				84.00									
6	Direct Ins.	04 1517	50.00								50.00					
7	J White	05 1518	100.00		100.00											
7	J Green	06 1519	200.00											200.00		
27	Bank charges	DD	250.00										250.00			
28	BT	23 1531	200.00									200.00				
	TOTAL		1784.00		100.00	100.00	84.00			800.00	50.00	200.00	250.00	200.00		
A	B	C	D	E	F	G	H	I	J	K	L	M	N	O	P	Q

Table 8 An example page from a cash book – payments

Note that direct and indirect costs have been grouped.

Column A	Enter the date. For simplicity you do not need to include the month and year as this appears at the top of the page.
Column B	The name of the person/company you have paid.
Column C	The reference number you have allocated to the invoice or entry followed by the last digits of the relevant cheque number.
Column D	The gross amount. The final total = columns E to P added together.
Column E	If VAT-registered you would enter the amount of VAT included in the gross amount. If not VAT-registered there is no need to include this.
Columns F – P	The amount broken down into appropriate headings. If VAT-registered these would be net amounts, i.e. the VAT-exclusive amount.
Column N	Any amount entered here needs to be identified in Row B as either bank charges, loan repayment or interest.
Column Q	Details of capital expenditure, i.e. details of the item purchased.

THE PETTY CASH BOOK

Most businesses will need a petty cash book and box. Within the box there should be a small book of petty cash vouchers (available from stationers). At the beginning of each period (probably each month) the amount of money in the box (the **float**) is noted in the petty cash book. The purposes of the petty cash book are:

1. The control of petty cash.
2. To keep records of small cash payments made.
3. To balance the petty cash.

Low-value payments which would clutter up the cash book are recorded in the petty cash book (also note that the bank will charge for every cheque processed, so paying very small amounts by cheque should be avoided). Petty cash payments may include small value purchases for the business, such as tea and coffee and miscellaneous stationery items.

Payments should only be made against the correct documentation, that is, a **petty cash voucher.** Receipts should be attached to the relevant petty cash voucher. If the business is VAT-registered and the cost of the item includes VAT, a proper VAT receipt should be requested and attached to the petty cash voucher. The petty cash should be replenished by drawing cash from the bank if necessary, or transferring cash from the cash book – receipts side.

<table>
<tr><td colspan="4" align="center">Petty Cash Voucher</td></tr>
<tr><td>Voucher No</td><td align="center">009</td><td>Date</td><td>25/02/10</td></tr>
<tr><td colspan="2" align="center">Item</td><td colspan="2" align="center">Amount
£   p</td></tr>
<tr><td colspan="2">Bart's Store – tea, milk and biscuits</td><td align="center">3</td><td align="center">52</td></tr>
<tr><td colspan="2">Total</td><td align="center">3</td><td align="center">52</td></tr>
<tr><td colspan="2">Approved by</td><td colspan="2" align="center">Nicola Smith</td></tr>
</table>

Table 9 An example petty cash voucher

At the beginning of the next month, the petty cash box should be topped-up to the amount you have decided to keep as your float.

> ITQ 64 Why might you show amounts for items on which VAT has been charged separately from items on which VAT has not been charged, even if these appear on the same supplier's invoice?

			Month: February Year: 2010				
Receipts	**Date**	**Voucher**	**Total**	**VAT**	**Office Supplies**	**Motor Exp.**	**Other**
50.00	7/2						
	23/2	008	11.75		11.75		
	25/2	009	3.52				3.52
	28/2	010	8.22			8.22	
50.00	**Total**		**23.49**		**11.75**	**8.22**	**3.52**
A			**B**	**C**	**D**	**E**	**F**

Table 10 An example page from a petty cash book

Column A   A £50 float in cash has been put into the petty cash. As this cash has come from sales this will appear on the receipts side of the cash book.

A – B = cash in the cash box = £50.00 – £23.49 = £26.51.

Column B   The total of C+D+E+F.
Column C   As the business is not VAT-registered, this column remains blank.
Columns D – F   The breakdown of individual amounts. If VAT-registered, these would be net amounts, i.e. the VAT-exclusive amounts.

ITQ 65 Give two reasons why a business might run a petty cash system:

1.

2.

BANK RECONCILIATION

At the end of each month (or more regularly if you use internet or PC banking), you must calculate the balance in your cash book and make sure that this agrees with the figures detailed on your monthly bank statement.

Conducting a monthly bank reconciliation will enable you to:

● Identify and correct any errors in your cash book.

- Identify and challenge with the bank any apparent errors in the bank statement.

Table 11 (page 65), which uses records of receipts and payments from Tables 6 and 8, shows how the above calculations would be shown. We have assumed an opening balance of £1,000 for the month.

If you have not already entered details of all the standing orders and direct debit payments which you have authorized your bank to make every month in the payments side of the cash book, refer to your bank statement and enter them now.

Similarly, if you receive any fees by standing order these should be entered into the receipts side of the cash book. Check the bank's details carefully – they do make mistakes. Once all of the entries for the month have been added to the relevant side of the cash book, your cash book balance can be calculated. To do this:

1. Take the balance as at the end of the previous month. We have assumed a balance of £1,000: (A) on Table 11.

2. Add all receipts for the month: (B) on Table 11.

3. Deduct the total payments made in the month: (D) on Table 11.

4. The resulting cash book balance includes the balance in the petty cash box (see Table 10): (E) on Table 11.

5. Deduct the petty cash balance: (F) on Table 11.

6. Compare the resulting total with the balance per the bank statement: (G and H) on Table 11.

The balance on the bank statement will rarely agree with your calculation. This can be a result of:

- Cheques made out to a supplier and entered in the cash book but not yet presented for payment by the supplier (**unpresented cheques**).

- Cheques (and sometimes cash) paid into the bank and entered in the cash book but not yet credited to your account (**cheques/cash in transit**). This may be a result of cash/cheques paid in towards the end of a working day not being shown on your account until the next working day.

7. Compare entries in your cash book and the bank statement.

8. Tick off entries in the cash book that appear on the bank statement – the entries not ticked in your cash book are those that the bank has not yet recorded.

9. Add up the payments-side entries that do not appear in the bank statement: (I) on Table 11.

10. Deduct them from the bank statement balance: (J) on Table 11.

11. Add up the receipts that do not appear on the bank statement: (K) on Table 11.

12. Add this to the total above: (J) on Table 11.

13. Provided you have not made mistakes, the figure in Row L should now agree with the total you think the bank balance should be: (G) on Table 11.

A	Cash book opening balance	£1000	
B	Plus cash receipts (from Table 6)	£1035	
C	Sub-total	£2035	A + B = C
D	Minus cash payments (from Table 8)	£1784	
E	Cash book balance	£251	C – D = E
F	Minus petty cash balance (from Table 10)	£26.51	
G	Cash in bank total	£224.49	E – F = G
H	Balance per bank statement	£344.49	
I	Deduct unpresented cheques 1531 £200.00 (See Row D Table 8)	£200.00	
J	Sub-total	£144.49	H – I = J
K	Add cash/cheques in transit 28/2/10 – banked £80.00 (See Row A Table 6)	£80.00	
L	Total	£224.49	J + K = L

Table 11 Example bank reconciliation

File your bank reconciliation with the relevant bank statement.

ITQ 66 Give two reasons for carrying out bank reconciliations:

1.

2.

ITQ 67 Why might your cash book balance and the bank statement balance disagree?

FINANCIAL FORECASTS

The financial forecast is first prepared in the planning stage of the business (business plan for the bank – see Chapter 1) and is ongoing once up and running. Financial forecasts enable you to manage the business finances, ensuring that sufficient funds are available to meet expected expenses. Forecasts may also be called for by a third party, for instance when applying for a bank loan. The main forecasts that should be kept up to date are the cash flow forecast and Income Statement (sometimes referred to as Profit and Loss Statements) forecast. To be of use, forecasts should be maintained by updating with actual spending and sales and adjusting predicted spending and sales if appropriate.

UPDATING THE CASH FLOW FORECAST

As previously mentioned, all financial forecasts have to be based to a certain extent on assumptions – reasonable estimates based on knowledge, experience and current information. This is obviously more difficult for a new business that does not have the benefit of previous records to go by. This is why for all businesses – especially new ones – good-quality market research is essential to ensure that robust/realistic assumptions can be used to produce these forecasts.

Established businesses are in a better position when forecasting the level of sales and expected costs as historical data can be used as a basis for calculations or to check calculations. For example, if estimated sales for a given period were significantly lower than the actual sales, the business could find itself in financial difficulty unless costs had been similarly reduced. It is therefore important to continually compare estimates with actual sales and costs and update financial forecasts to reflect significant adverse or favourable variances, so that the managers are armed with information to make decisions quickly about issues and plan the business's future (short-, medium- and long-term).

At least monthly, compare the figures in your cash book with your latest cash flow forecast and update the projections for future months to take account of changes in circumstances. Changes in the business or its local position could account for the decrease in sales over that forecast. These might include:

- A new competitor opening unexpectedly.
- Fewer horses or staff being available than had been expected.
- Less effective marketing than had been anticipated.
- Seasonal adjustments that had not been reflected in the original forecasts

This emphasizes the importance of conducting thorough research before starting the business, keeping informed about competition and continuing with effective marketing whilst trading. If the cash flow forecast is kept up to date, you will be able to use these figures to produce a current Income Statement (Profit and Loss Statements) forecast.

CHAPTER SUMMARY

This chapter has explained how to keep income and expenditure records for the business. These records can then be used to produce forecasts to aid financial management of the business. Effective day-to-day financial management is essential if the business is to have a chance of surviving its first few years of trading. Cash flow must be particularly closely managed. For simplicity we have assumed the business is not VAT-registered. This is fairly true to life as most new equestrian businesses do not need to be VAT-registered at first.

The next chapter deals with the way in which VAT accounts are kept.

CHAPTER 3

VAT ACCOUNTING

The aims and objectives of this chapter are to explain:

- The difference between input tax and output tax.
- Records to be kept for VAT purposes.
- How to calculate the amount of VAT included in a price or to be added to a price.
- How to account for VAT in the book-keeping system.
- How to prepare a quarterly VAT summary.

The details provided within this chapter are intended as a guide as to how VAT affects the way in which a small business would keep financial records. Certain areas of VAT are complicated and advice should always be sought from your accountant and the VAT office when appropriate. At the time of writing, the VAT office can be contacted for assistance on 0845 010 9000.

VAT is one of the forms of indirect taxation administered by HM Revenue and Customs. Other major forms of indirect taxation administered by this body include:

- **Stamp duty** – payable when purchasing houses and on leases.

- **Customs and excise duties** – payable on imports and exports (excise duties are also payable on goods such as alcohol, tobacco, petrol and diesel).

Stamp duty and customs and excise duties are not normally primary concerns of small businesses which do not import or export, so in this chapter we will concentrate on VAT. Do however seek the advice of your solicitor or accountant as to the effects of stamp duty on any lease you may be intending to take out for business premises.

VAT TERMS AND BASIC REQUIREMENTS

We will start by looking at the terms used when talking about VAT.

VAT-registered businesses are given a **VAT Registration Number**, which is shown on most business paperwork including invoices, receipts and headed paper.

When registered for VAT, the business charges tax to clients on taxable supplies and services. This is known as **output tax**. The business may claim back VAT charged to it by others. This is known as **input tax**.

Common practice relating to this works as follows. In theory, all VAT-registered businesses charge the tax on the value that the business has added to the item or service being supplied – hence Value Added Tax. This means that, theoretically, if Mr Fixit Plumbing Services fixed a new sink into your premises, he would charge VAT on his costs only and not on the cost of the sink which he had purchased – the value he had added being installing the sink. In practice what happens is that Mr Fixit charges VAT on the full cost of supplying and fitting and then reclaims the VAT he has paid on the cost of the sink from the VAT office. In terms of your equestrian business, you must seek the advice of your accountant when determining how to calculate the VAT you should charge.

If your business is VAT-registered, you will be able to claim back input tax on purchases which relate to the business. These may include office equipment, the telephone bill and payments for business services, such as accountants, solicitors, farrier and vet.

However, depending upon the legislation in force at a particular time, there are items for which the VAT may not be claimed back. These currently include company cars and supplies for business entertainment. Note that VAT rules are often different from Inland Revenue rules regarding deductions of taxes.

HM Revenue and Customs will decide when your quarterly VAT returns will be due and may require the first return to cover a period of greater, or less, than the usual 3 months. You can apply to HM Revenue and Customs for your VAT return dates to be changed, e.g. so that they coincide with your financial year.

KEEPING VAT RECORDS

All registered businesses must keep the following records for a minimum of 6 years:

- Orders and delivery notes.
- Relevant business correspondence.
- Purchase and sales books.
- Cash books and other accounting books.
- Purchase invoices and copy sales invoices.
- Records of daily takings.
- Annual accounts including profit and loss accounts.
- Import and export documents.
- Bank statements and paying-in slips.
- VAT accounts.
- Credit/debit notes issued or received.

Occasionally a VAT officer will arrange to visit the business premises and go through all records, so it is important that they are kept in accordance with the requirements.

CALCULATING VAT

When calculating the amount of VAT in a VAT-inclusive cost (assuming VAT is at 17.5 per cent):

$$\frac{\text{VAT-inclusive cost} \times 7}{47} = \text{amount of VAT included}$$

$$\text{For example,} \ \frac{£117.50 \times 7}{47} = £17.50$$

The VAT included in an item costing £117.50 is therefore £17.50. Alternatively, if the VAT rate changes, the following general formula could be used:

$$\frac{\text{VAT-inclusive cost} \times \ \text{percentage rate of VAT (i.e. 17.5)}}{(100 + \text{rate of VAT})} = \text{amount of VAT included}$$

When calculating how much VAT to *add on* to *VAT-exclusive* cost:

$$\frac{\text{VAT-exclusive cost} \times 17.5}{100} = \text{amount of VAT to add}$$

Or, more generally:

$$\frac{\text{VAT-exclusive cost} \times \text{percentage rate of VAT (i.e. 17.5)}}{100} = \text{amount of VAT to add}$$

$$\text{For example,} \ \frac{£100 \times 17.5}{100} = £17.50$$

ITQ 68 Calculate the VAT included in the following VAT-inclusive prices, assuming that VAT is at the standard rate of 17.5%:

a. £76.37

b. £169.20

c. £675.62

ITQ 69 Calculate the amount of VAT payable on the following VAT-exclusive (or net) prices, again assuming that VAT is at 17.5%:

a. £11.55

b. £10.00

c. £70.00

ITQ 70 List five of the records that a business must keep for a minimum of six years:

1.

2.

3.

4.

5.

ITQ 71 Why do businesses have to keep these records for such a length of time?

VAT ACCOUNTING DOCUMENTS AND PRACTICES

In order to satisfy the requirements of HM Revenue and Customs when making claims for repayment of VAT or detailing the amount of VAT to be paid by the business, copies of tax invoices for all sales and payments must be maintained.

TAX INVOICES

In general, except as detailed later for retail sales, tax invoices must include the following details:

1. The supplier's name, address and VAT registration number.
2. An identifying invoice number.
3. Details of the items or services supplied.
4. The customer's name and address.
5. The tax point.
6. The net amount.
7. The VAT rate and amount.
8. The gross amount.

Tax Points

As stated, tax invoices must include the tax point. The tax point is the date on which a liability to HM Revenue and Customs is established and may be either:

ITQ 72 Why is Value Added Tax so called?

ITQ 73

a. With reference to a VAT invoice, what is the basic tax point?

b. What is the actual tax point?

ITQ 74

a. What does the Cash Accounting Scheme allow?

b. What advantage would there be to a small business in joining the Cash Accounting Scheme?

ITQ 75 When would a business be eligible to join the Annual Accounting Scheme?

ITQ 76 What is input tax?

ITQ 77 What is output tax?

Second-hand Goods (Margin) Scheme

Another scheme which may be applicable to those within the equestrian industry is the second-hand goods scheme, also called the Margin Scheme. VAT on second-hand goods is chargeable on the profit made when selling the goods rather than the total sales price. An example of this would be when a VAT-registered business was to sell a horse or pony. Say, for example, the pony was bought for £500 and later sold for £800 – a profit of £300. The VAT payable under the second-hand goods scheme would be £52.50 (17.5% of £300).

Businesses can elect to join the above schemes if they meet the criteria for doing so. It would always be worth seeking the advice of your accountant or the VAT office as to whether it would be in the long-term interest of the business to join such a scheme.

RECORDING SALES

To comply with the requirements of HM Revenue and Customs when recording sales, the following steps must be taken:

1. Issue tax invoices for all standard-rated sales unless using one of the retailing schemes. HM Revenue and Customs publish leaflets giving detailed information about these schemes. Most of the sales of an organization such as an equestrian centre would be recorded under one of these schemes.

2. Issue invoices which show the same information as tax invoices for any zero-rated or exempt sales made (for instance if selling feed or hay).

3. Keep copies of all invoices and do a summary of them.

As mentioned earlier, invoices issued to clients should be numbered. The number must be recorded against the payment when entered into the daily receipts diary. For ease of reference, paid sales invoices should be filed by invoice number. For most equine businesses, the sales record within the cash book would be used as the basis for calculating a VAT sales summary for the VAT return. This would show the following separate totals:

1. VAT on sales.
2. Sales exclusive of VAT.
3. Exempt sales.

Table 13 overleaf shows how VAT is recorded on sales.

RECORDING PURCHASES

All of the necessary details will be shown on the supplier's tax invoices and will have been entered into the cash book payments side on a daily basis. The summary of purchases for the VAT return would be prepared from the payments side of the cash book.

Date	Details	A Bank	B Cheques	C Cash	D VAT	E Livery	F Lessons	G Other Amount	G Other Details
3.2.10	Daily receipts diary (See Table 5)		464.12	35.25	74.37	300.00	105.00	20.00	Hire indoor school
4.2.10	Banked	499.37							
6.2.10	Daily receipts diary		117.50	58.75	26.25		110.00	40.00	Clipping
7.2.10	Daily receipts diary		352.50	94.00	66.50	300.00	80.00		
7.2.10	To petty cash	50.00							
7.2.10	Banked	572.75							
28.2.10	Daily receipts diary		23.50	70.50	14.00		80.00		
28.2.10	Banked	94.00							
	TOTAL	1216.12	957.62	258.50	181.12	600.00	375.00	60.00	

Table 13 Example receipts page from a cash book of a VAT-registered business

This table is based on Table 6. The net figures are the same but show how the receipts page will look should the business become VAT registered.

Column A   The total banked. The figures in this column should match your paying-in book slips (minus any amount put into petty cash). This figure is reached by adding together Rows B and C above. Note that sales from 6.2.10 and 7.2.10 amounted to £622.75. £50 of this was put into petty cash and £572.75 was banked.

Column B   All cheques received for VAT-inclusive sales.

Column C   All cash received for VAT-inclusive sales.

Column D   As this business is VAT-registered, VAT is shown separately.

Column E   Livery payments excluding VAT. Of the £425 (net) received on 3 February, £300 was made up of livery fees.

Column F   Lesson payments excluding VAT. Of the £425 (net) received on 3 February, £105.00 was made up of lessons.

Column G   Other receipts excluding VAT. Of the £425 (net) received on 3 February, £20 was for hire of the indoor school.

Separate totals would be shown for:

1. VAT you have been charged on purchases.
2. Value of purchases exclusive of VAT.

Keep separate records of any business purchases from which you cannot deduct input tax, such as cars and business entertainment expenses.

Table 14 (page 73) is based on Table 8. It has been adapted to show how it would look if the business were to become VAT-registered. Note that not all of the purchased items or services attract VAT. This means that the total VAT shown in the VAT column (Column E), will not be 17.5% of the total net sales (Columns F – P added together).

PREPARING THE QUARTERLY VAT ACCOUNT OR SUMMARY

A VAT account is a summary of the totals of output and input tax for each tax period. A VAT period is normally quarterly – you can agree your quarter dates with your local VAT office. The amount of VAT to be paid to HM Revenue and Customs (or refundable by HM Revenue and Customs) would be calculated as the difference between the output tax and input tax during the period.

Deduct the total input tax from the total output tax to calculate the amount of VAT payable. A negative result, meaning that you have paid out more VAT than you have collected, would mean that you could claim the amount back from the VAT office.

The VAT *sales summary* for one quarter (three-month period) for an equestrian centre might look like this:

	Gross sales £	VAT £	Net sales £
Month 1	1,216.12	181.12	1,035.00
Month 2	1,762.50	262.50	1,500.00
Month 3	2,350.00	350.00	2,000.00
Totals	**5,328.62**	**793.62**	**4,535.00**

The total output tax for this quarter would be £793.62.

The VAT *payment summary* for one quarter for an equestrian centre might look like this:

	Gross payments £	VAT £	Net payments £
Month 1	1,851.20	67.20	1,784.00
Month 2	1,148.75	148.75	1,000.00
Month 3	2,437.50	237.50	2,200.00
Totals	**5,437.45**	**453.45**	**4,984.00**

The total input tax for this quarter would be £453.45.

Total output tax	£793.62
less total input tax	£453.45
VAT payable/due	£340.17

In this example, £340.17 is payable to HM Revenue and Customs.

Month: February   Year: 2010

					Direct costs						Indirect costs				Capital expenditure	
Date	Details	Ref. Chq No.	Total	V A T	Wages	Feed, hay, bedding	Farrier Vet	Motor exp.	Advert	Rent Utilities	Insurance	Office Phone	Bank charges Loan	Drawings	Amount	Details
2	Hiscock Farms Ltd	01 1514	800.00							800.00						
3	Brown Feeds*	02 1515	117.50	17.50		100.00										
5	M Black Farrier*	03 1516	98.70	14.70			84.00									
6	Direct Ins.	04 1517	50.00								50.00					
7	J White	05 1518	100.00		100.00											
7	J Green	06 1519	200.00											200.00		
27	Bank charges	DD	250.00										250.00			
28	BT*	23 1531	235.00	35.00								200.00				
	TOTAL		1851.20	67.20	100.00	100.00	84.00			800.00	50.00	200.00	250.00	200.00		
A	B	C	D	E	F	G	H	I	J	K	L	M	N	O	P	Q

Table 14 Example payments page from a cash book of a VAT-registered business

Column B   The name of the person/company you have paid. Those with an asterisk are VAT-registered. Note that the feed supplier will only charge VAT on bedding. In this example the invoice for £100 was for paper bedding. VAT is not payable on horse feed or hay.

Column D   The gross amount (including VAT). The final total = columns E to P added together.

Column E   The VAT included in the gross amount.

Columns F–P The amount broken down into appropriate headings. As this business is VAT-registered these are net amounts, i.e. the VAT-exclusive amounts.

Remember:

VAT deductible (input tax)	**VAT payable (output tax)**
VAT on purchases	VAT on sales
Errors in earlier returns	Errors in earlier returns

The VAT return and payment must be sent no later than one month after the end of the tax period. A leaflet, issued by HM Revenue and Customs entitled *Filling in Your VAT Return*, will help you to do this.

ITQ 78 Use the figures in the table below as the basis for a quarterly VAT return. Calculate how much VAT would have to be paid to, or refunded by, HM Revenue and Customs. Assume that VAT on all sales is at 17.5%.

Net sales		
	Month 1	£5,520
	Month 2	£4,350
	Month 3	£7,590

Net payments	Month 1	Month 2	Month 3
Hay and Feed	£500	£400	£300
Wages	£500	£500	£500
Bedding	£400	£0	£200
Vet	£200	£85	£175
Farrier	£100	£145	£200
Advertising	£75	£150	£200
Rent	£800	£800	£800
Bank charges	£100	£0	£0

Assume that:

1. The business has made no other payments in the period concerned.
2. All suppliers are VAT-registered but note that hay and feed, wages, rent and bank charges will not attract VAT.

	Gross sales £	VAT (output) £	Net sales £
Month 1			
Month 2			
Month 3			
Totals			
	Gross payments £	VAT (input) £	Net payments £
Month 1			
Month 2			
Month 3			
Totals			

Total output tax:

Less total input tax:

VAT payable/due:

VAT-EXEMPT ACTIVITIES IN THE EQUESTRIAN INDUSTRY

When calculating the turnover of a business to find out if it has reached the VAT threshold, *VAT-exempt* activities do not have to be included. The VAT threshold does not apply to total turnover but to total *taxable* turnover, i.e. sales that are standard, reduced or zero-rated.

Exempt Rights Over Land

Most livery services, e.g. mucking out, grooming, feeding, exercising and arranging veterinary treatment carry the standard rate of VAT.

However, in relation to **exempt rights over land** there are some exceptions to this with regard to stabling. If a horse owner is granted exclusive use of a particular stable in the yard as part of the livery agreement, this can be treated as a VAT-exempt supply of land. Under these circumstances you do not have to charge VAT to the horse's owner on anything you supply in the livery package. Likewise you cannot claim back VAT on anything you supply.

This is an optional arrangement – you *can* charge VAT on the rented part of the stable and then claim the VAT back on items purchased to service it. If the latter option is chosen you have to do so for a minimum of 20 years.

Horse feed is zero-rated, so hay, cereals and other feeds do not carry VAT if sold to external clients. However, if they are provided as part of a livery service, they are standard-rated for VAT. They can only be zero-rated when no element of care is supplied by you, e.g. if you are selling them to a DIY livery client or if the stabling is an exempt right over land that you have opted not to tax.

Provided they are not part of a livery agreement that is subject to VAT, grass and grazing rights are also zero-rated.

Tuition Provided Personally by the Sole Proprietor of a Riding School

Income derived from tuition supplied by the proprietor (or, in the case of a partnership, one of the partners) can be deducted from the total income of the school, which may bring the income below the VAT threshold. This exemption does not apply to tuition delivered by employees or directors of a limited company.

Income from Training Ultimately Funded by the Government

Certain vocational training schemes and training provided on behalf of a college that is funded by the Government are normally classified as VAT-exempt services.

All VAT-exempt services should be added together and deducted from the business's total income.

CHAPTER SUMMARY

This chapter has expanded upon the information given in Chapter 1 – Business Planning. The concept of VAT accounting should be relatively simple to implement once the principles of book-keeping are understood. As with all aspects of record-keeping, the more up to date you keep your records, the less data you have to deal with at any one time. This makes the whole prospect of VAT accounting less daunting. The worst (and fairly common) situation is when the book-keeping slips and there are hundreds of entries to be made. This makes the whole prospect more unpleasant so the process becomes even more of a chore.

With respect to VAT in the equestrian industry, keep abreast of legislative developments – The British Horse Society provides information and assistance regarding VAT specific to the horse industry and there are frequently news pieces in magazines such as *Horse and Hound*.

In the next chapter we will look at the annual financial statements, otherwise known as the annual accounts.

CHAPTER 4

THE ANNUAL FINANCIAL STATEMENTS

The aims and objectives of this chapter are to explain:

- The basic principles of the annual financial statements.
- The figures used by the accountant to make up the trading and profit and loss accounts.
- The figures used as a basis for the balance sheet.
- How the business's tax liabilities are calculated from the accounts.
- The outline principles of self-assessment.
- How the business pays its tax.

Annual financial statements, also called the **end of year accounts,** are prepared by the accountant at the end of your financial year. Having a basic understanding of how they are prepared and what the resulting figures mean will help you make informed financial decisions.

As explained in earlier chapters, it is important to consider the categories of expenditure by which you will manage the business and to seek the accountant's advice when setting up these systems. This will mean that the figures contained within the financial statements prepared by the accountant can easily be cross-referred to the figures within your cash book and other financial records.

The annual financial statements prepared by your accountant will include:

- A trading account.
- A profit and loss account.
- A balance sheet.

All figures in the annual financial statements will exclude VAT if the business is VAT-registered. This is because any VAT charged must be paid over to HM Revenue and Customs and therefore does not form part of the sales figures, and VAT included in costs is claimed back by the business so it does not form a cost to the business.

If the business is not VAT-registered, VAT *is* included in the costs as it does form a genuine cost to the business. This is because the business cannot claim it back from HM Revenue and Customs.

> **Note:** On 1 January 2005 a new set of international accounting standards were introduced named IFRS (International Financial Reporting Standards). In summary this means that the way in which financial statements are reported has changed to incorporate new terminology; for example, the Profit and Loss statement is now referred to as an Income Statement, and Fixed Assets as Non-current Assets. There are other changes to the Cash Flow Statement, including that it is mandatory to produce a cash flow statement under the new regulations, even for small businesses. IFRS reporting was initially only introduced for large companies on listed markets, but in January 2007 these standards were rolled out to AIM (Alternative Investment Market) listed companies. Currently it is only choice as to whether a small business adopts IFRS for its reporting; however your accountant will advise you if this changes in the future.

THE TRADING AND PROFIT AND LOSS ACCOUNTS
THE TRADING ACCOUNT

The main purpose of the trading account is to identify the sales margin over cost, or the total gross profit. It shows the total sales less direct costs adjusted for changes in stock value between the start and end of the financial period. This equals the gross profit.

In reality, the gross profit figure will have little meaning to the equestrian business as it makes no allowance for indirect costs (i.e. overheads). The trading account and profit and loss account are generally prepared as part of one financial statement.

THE PROFIT AND LOSS ACCOUNT

The profit and loss account for the business expands upon the trading account by including indirect costs. A computerized accounting system will enable you to periodically (monthly or quarterly) prepare financial statements, including profit and loss accounts, literally at the press of a button. These are usually referred to as **management accounts** and help in the financial management of the business.

The accountant will prepare the annual financial statements for the business using records provided by the business. These records include:

- Bank statements and associated cheque books and paying-in books.
- The cash book.
- Any other records of receipts or payments made.
- Records of invoices outstanding to suppliers (creditors).
- Records of invoices outstanding with clients (debtors).

If you are using a computer system, the accountant can use the actual files on disk to prepare the accounts.

If you have developed your record systems to clearly identify all of the main sources of income and expenditure and have consulted with your accountant when doing so, he or she will easily be able to summarize that information in the profit and loss account. The profit and loss account will include all entries in the cash book, with the exception of capital expenditure, drawings and repayment of liabilities and loans.

- Capital expenditure, creditors and debtors are included in the balance sheet.

- Depreciation of assets is shown on the balance sheet and on the profit and loss account.

- Drawings taken by the business owner (sole trader or partnership) are shown as part of the capital calculation in the balance sheet. Drawings are not shown as a cost to the business in the profit and loss account, whereas wages are.

- Repayment of liabilities will be shown in the balance sheet.

- Interest paid on a loan is shown as an indirect cost on the profit and loss account.

Your accountant will calculate the amount of income tax and National Insurance Contributions (NICs) that are payable on the net profit made by the business. Income Tax and NICs are covered in more detail in the next chapter.

Example trading and profit and loss accounts for an equestrian centre for its first financial year are shown in Table 15.

ITQ 79 Name the three main financial statements that usually form part of your annual accounts:

1.

2.

3.

ITQ 80 What is the main purpose of the trading account?

	TRADING ACCOUNT	£
A	Total sales revenue	21, 000
B	Direct costs of sales	9,600
C	Plus – opening value of stock	Nil
D	Less – closing value of stock	2,500
E	**Gross profit**	**13, 900**

	PROFIT AND LOSS ACCOUNT	
	Indirect costs	£
F	Motor expenses	750
G	Advertising	400
H	Rent and utilities	9,600
I	Insurance	600
J	Office and phone	1,000
K	Repairs and renewals	600
L	Bank charges and interest	300
M	Depreciation	1,390
N	**Total indirect costs**	**14, 640**
O	**Net profit (loss)**	**£ (740)**

Table 15 Example trading and profit and loss accounts

Remember:

Cost of sales = direct costs + opening stock – closing stock: B + C – D = £7100

Gross profit = sales revenue – cost of sales: A – (B + C – D) £21, 000 – £7,100 = £13, 900

Row A	12 months' sales exclusive of VAT taken from the cash book. This ties in with the sales in the cash flow forecast (Table 1).
Row B	12 months' direct costs of sales exclusive of VAT taken from the cash book. This ties in with the direct costs in the cash flow forecast (Table 1).
Row C	As this was a new business, it had no opening stock.
Row D	The value of hay, straw, etc. remaining in stock at the end of the year. This figure will also be used as the opening stock value for the next financial year. You must prepare a list of all stock to prove stock levels.
Row E	Gross profit.
Rows F – K	12 months' indirect costs exclusive of VAT.
Row L	Comprises interest on the bank loan and charges made by the bank based on the number and type of transactions made.
Row M	Depreciation on horses, equipment and leasehold improvements taken from the balance sheet (Table 16).
Row N	12 months' indirect costs exclusive of VAT.
Row O	Net profit or loss. Gross profit minus indirect costs (Row E minus Row N). This business has made a small trading loss in its first year.

ITQ 81 Indicate in which financial statements the following items are shown:

Capital expenditure

Creditors and debtors

Repayment of liabilities

Drawings

Depreciation

Interest on a loan

Staff wages

.

THE BALANCE SHEET

The balance sheet prepared as part of the annual financial statements shows the assets of the business against the capital and liabilities and represents the value of the business at the end of the financial year. The value of assets shown on the balance sheet will:

- Increase as capital expenditure is made.

- Decrease as time passes, because of depreciation.

- Fluctuate as account sales are made and debtors' invoices paid.

The value of liabilities shown on the balance sheet will:

- Increase as loans are taken.

- Decrease as loan repayments are made.

- Increase with the value of invoices received from suppliers but not paid.

- Decrease as payment to creditors is made.

DEPRECIATION

The value of fixed assets owned by the business is usually written off over the period of time in which they would be expected to last. For instance, a new computer system might be expected to need replacing after as little as

3 years (technological advances often make systems obsolete quite quickly). In such a case the value of the asset would be depreciated by one third of its cost for each of the 3 years after it is purchased.

Buildings are generally depreciated over 10 years and motor vehicles over 5 years. If in any doubt as to how depreciation will affect the value of your assets, seek the advice of your accountant. HM Revenue and Customs provides specific guidelines governing rates of depreciation.

The opening balance sheet at Table 3 (page 44) detailed the value of assets and liabilities at the start of business for an example equestrian centre. A bank loan of £5,000 was taken out in Month 1 to help finance the set-up costs. The loan is repayable over 5 years.

Further capital expenditure was made in the first year as detailed on page 44. These purchases would increase the value of equipment owned by the business by the total cost of the items.

Value of horses and equipment at start of business (see Table 3)	=	£5,950
Plus capital purchase/leasehold improvements	=	£5,950
Total value of equipment	=	**£11,900**

It is also worth noting that, whether horses will be seen as a fixed asset on the balance sheet, or whether the cost of buying them will be shown as a direct cost of sale on the profit and loss account, will depend on their purpose. If bought to school and sell on, the cost would be shown as a direct cost of sale. If used to generate revenue, e.g. for use in lessons, the value of the horse will be shown as a fixed asset. If you sell a horse who was bought to generate revenue, this would be reflected in a decrease in the value of your fixed assets.

The balance sheet forming part of the annual financial statement at the end of the first year's trading for our example equestrian centre is shown in Table 16 overleaf.

> ITQ 82 How would it affect the annual financial statements if the business paid all outstanding debts before the end of the financial year?
>
> 1.
>
> 2.
>
> 3.

		£	£
	FIXED ASSETS		
A	Horses	3,000	
B	Less depreciation	450	2,550
C	Tack and equipment	2,950	
	Less depreciation	440	2,510
D	Leasehold improvements	5,950	
	Less depreciation	500	5,450
			10, 510 (1)
	CURRENT ASSETS		
E	Stock	2,500	
F	Debtors	500	
G	Cash at bank	–	**3,000 (2)**
	CURRENT LIABILITIES		
H	Creditors	500	
I	Overdraft	6,000	**6,500 (3)**
	Net current assets/ (liabilities)		**(3,500) (4) = (2) – (3)**
	LONG-TERM LIABILITIES		
J	Bank loan		**4,200 (5)**
	NET ASSETS		**£2,810 (6) = (1) – (4) – (5)**
	FINANCED BY		
K	Opening balance		Nil
L	Capital introduced		6,950
M	Loss for year		(740)
N	Less drawings		3,400
O	**FUNDS EMPLOYED**		**£2,810**

Table 16 An example balance sheet – end of year one

Notes on the balance sheet figures:

Row A Horses – from the opening balance sheet – Table 3.

Row B The value of the horses will be depreciated over approximately 7 years. £450 = approximately one seventh of £3000 (rounded up).

Row C Tack and equipment – £2,950 from the opening balance sheet – Table 3.

Row D Leasehold improvements – taken from Row S of the cash flow (Table 1). Additional equipment purchased and improvements to the premises.

(1)   Total value of the fixed assets.

Row E   Stock – taken from the trading and profit and loss accounts, Table 15. This is likely to be hay, straw and bedding materials. Note that you must make an accurate list itemizing all stock to prove your stock levels.

Row F   The business has debtors – clients who have been invoiced for their livery and lessons but have yet to pay.

Row G   There is no cash at the bank as the business has an overdraft.

(2)   The total of current assets.

Row H   The business owes £500 to suppliers.

Row I   The overdraft facility.

(3)   The total of current liabilities.

(4)   Net current assets (2) – (3).

Row J (5) We have assumed that £800 (excluding interest) has been paid off the original bank loan of £5,000.

(6)   Net assets (1) – (4) – (5).

Row K   As this was a new business the opening balance was nil.

Row L   As seen on the opening balance sheet (Table 3) the owner introduced capital of £6,950.

Row M   The loss for the year is taken from the trading and profit and loss account (Table 15).

DIRECT TAX LIABILITIES

With respect to running a business, there are two main types of direct taxation: **income tax** and **corporation tax**.

INCOME TAX

This is collected in two ways:

1. **Pay as You Earn**. The employer has to obtain income tax and National Insurance contributions from the staff on behalf of the Government.

2. **Schedule D.** The taxing of profits from trade.

Self Assessment

The system of Self Assessment has been in operation since 1996. Self-employed persons, whether sole traders or partners, receive a **tax return** in the April of every year. The system purports to be a straightforward and efficient way of working out tax. However, it is strongly recommended that you seek the advice of your accountant when filling in Self Assessment tax returns. Generally, your tax bill will be based on your trading profits for the accounting year. However, at the start of a new business, special rules apply. The tax office will advise as to the period for which you will be taxed.

- In the first year of business you will be taxed on the profits for the period from the date you started trading to the following 5 April.

- For the second year you are taxed on the profits of the 12 months to your accounting date in that year, provided that date falls 12 months or more after the date on which you started business.

- If your accounting date in the second year falls less than 12 months after the date on which you started the business, you will be taxed instead on the profits of the first 12 months of business.

- For the third year you are taxed on the profits for your accounting year.

These periods may involve a degree of overlap. There is an adjustment called **'overlap relief'** which is used at the end of your business (i.e. when the business ceases to trade) to make sure that at no time have you paid too much (or too little) tax.

Paying Tax

Under Self Assessment you will receive your tax return in April every year. You must complete this, giving the information needed to work out your tax bill. You then have two options:

1. Complete the tax return and calculate your tax bill yourself (with the help of your accountant). This must be sent to HM Revenue and Customs by 31 October.

2. Ask HM Revenue and Customs to calculate your bill. The completed tax return must be sent to HM Revenue and Customs by 31 October.

The tax return also explains how to calculate any Class 4 National Insurance contributions that are due. After the first year of business you are required to make two payments on account towards your tax bill each year. The first payment is made on January 31 and the second on July 31. Any balance due is made on the following January 31 along with the first payment on account for the following year.

You should set aside money regularly so you can pay your tax and NICs when they become due. Late payment incurs interest and sometimes a fine.

If you make a loss you may be able to set it against any other taxable income you have, or the loss can be carried forward to offset your profits in later years.

Under Self Assessment you do not have to send your annual accounts to the Tax Office with your tax return. There is a special section on the return for you to fill in your accounting information. The Tax Office may ask to see your annual accounts if they want to check the figures in your return. They will do this within 12 months of receiving your Self Assessment.

CORPORATION TAX

Corporation tax is the tax payable by limited companies, assessed under Schedule D. When a limited company is formed the directors draw a salary and are taxed on this salary as employees (i.e. PAYE). The salaries and associated PAYE and NICs are classified as costs to the business.

The company's tax liability, i.e. the amount of corporation tax it owes, is based on the amount of profit made. An annual return is completed and sent to HM Revenue and Customs with a copy of the annual accounts. The tax owed is paid in one lump sum 9 months after the business's financial year ends.

An abbreviated version of the accounts, i.e. the balance sheet and relevant notes, will be sent to the Registrar of Companies at Companies House. Only the full accounts of very large limited companies exceeding a specified turnover need to be audited.

The directors of the company complete individual tax returns. A proportion of the company's profit can be taken by each director as a **dividend**. As tax has already been paid on the company's profit, dividends are not taxable. Dividends are *not* classified as a cost to the business, so do not affect the profit level.

CHAPTER SUMMARY

As our veterinary books do not attempt to teach you to become a vet, so this book and the chapters within do not attempt to teach you to become an accountant! These are specialist professions with regulated qualifications that take years of training and expertise to achieve.

What this chapter has attempted to do is give you an overview and basic knowledge of what the accountant does. It has been prepared in a simplified manner for that purpose. The accountant will advise you on specific queries. To run an equestrian business successfully you do not need to be an accountant but you do need to know how to manage the records on a daily basis so that the accountant's job is easier at the end of the year. This makes good financial sense, as you then won't have to pay the accountant as much as if the record-keeping is poor and incorrect.

Most farms and equestrian businesses employ a book-keeper – there are many who work on a freelance part-time basis, which provides the flexibility needed by a young, growing business.

CHAPTER 5

EMPLOYING AND PAYING STAFF

The aims and objectives of this chapter are to explain:

- The main legal duties of the employer and the employee.

- The main rights and obligations of the employer.

- The main rights and obligations of the employee.

- The paperwork necessary when taking on an employee.

- The principles of Pay as You Earn (PAYE) and National Insurance Contributions (NICs).

- The basic requirements of Statutory Sick Pay (SSP) and Statutory Maternity Pay (SMP).

Health and safety issues and insurance requirements will be covered in Chapter 6.

Most businesses at some stage employ staff. Employment law changes continuously and rapidly. This is not only because of new legislation (much of it driven by the European Union) but also because the way legislation is interpreted is continuously being developed and changed by the courts to cope with new situations and changing employment practices.

This chapter is therefore only a very general guide to some of the most common employment law areas.

You will be able to keep abreast of relevant changes by watching current affairs programmes dealing with pertinent subjects and reading related articles in newspapers. The Department for Business, Innovation and Skills web site at www.berr.gov.uk also includes links to useful documents. Although details provided within this chapter are correct as at June 2009, changes to the law occur regularly. It is therefore important that you use the media to keep abreast of relevant changes.

In the Introduction to this book, the point was made that legislation and associated practices vary from country to country, and that this book focuses on what is applicable to the UK. So far as employment law is concerned, in most cases legislation is applicable to equestrian businesses in England, Wales, Scotland and Northern Ireland. However, legislation relating to Scotland and Northern Ireland is contained in different statutory instruments and employment law in these areas may differ.

The information provided within this chapter is intended as a general guide to the main requirements of employment law and should not be used in place of professional legal advice. Employers (and employees) should always take legal advice on their own specific circumstances from either a solicitor or Citizens' Advice Bureau.

THE LEGAL SYSTEM – A GENERAL OUTLINE

The English legal system is based upon a combination of **statute** and **common law** and is also affected by **EU Regulations and Directives**. The European Union came into effect on 1 November 1993, with the signing of the Maastricht Treaty.

- **Statute law** (or **legislation**) is made up of **Acts of Parliament** and **subordinate legislation** (rules devised by, for instance, the Government under authority of Parliament – including **Statutory Instruments**).

- **Common law** – also known as the **doctrine of precedent**, can be defined as 'the practice whereby a previous decision of a court may be binding on future courts in a similar case'. Common law is therefore based mainly on legal precedents – the results of previous cases – and is sometimes referred to as **case law**.

Another distinction in the English legal system is between **civil** and **criminal law**. Both are made up of statute and common law – although criminal law is more closely tied to legislation than is civil law.

The following are very general definitions of civil and criminal law:

- **Civil law** cases are brought before the **County Court** by an individual (the **claimant**) against another individual (the **defendant**).

- **Criminal law** cases are prosecuted on behalf of the State by the **Director of Public Prosecutions** and are heard by **Magistrates** or **Crown Courts**.

With respect to employment, an employee might bring a grievance against an employer (or vice versa) for contravening the requirements of the legislation (and precedents) forming employment law in a civil case. Such cases are heard in the civil courts or Employment Tribunals, depending on the type of case involved.

An employer may also be open to prosecution by the State for contravening requirements of employment law and could, in such a case, face criminal charges.

DEFINING AN EMPLOYEE

Not everyone who carries out work for you is an 'employee'. Some people will work for you in a self-employed capacity. It is important to understand the difference between the two categories of workers as, generally speaking, an employee has more legal rights than a self-employed worker.

The relationship between you and someone working for you in a self-employed capacity is purely a contractual one. The self-employed person, a farrier for instance, will have agreed to carry out a task or range of tasks for you and you will have agreed to pay them a sum of money in consideration. You have not agreed to 'employ' that person and the relationship between you is not one of employer and employee. The requirements of employment law will consequently not apply to such an arrangement.

You cannot, however, simply decide that, in order to avoid having to comply with employment law, you will take all your workers on in a self-employed capacity. The courts, HM Revenue and Customs (HMRC) and Employment Tribunals will not automatically agree with what the 'employer' says the status of the worker is. They will make their own decision considering such things as:

- How much control the 'employer' has over the worker. The more control the worker has over such things as how and when he or she works, the more likely the worker is to be seen as self-employed. Conversely, the more control the 'employer' has, the more likely it is that the worker will be considered as employed.

- Whether the worker is an integral part of the organization.

- Whether the worker provides his or her own equipment. If so, the worker is more likely to be seen as self-employed.

- Whether the worker hires his or her own helpers. Again, if so, this may indicate self-employed status.

- If the worker takes a degree of financial risk.

- Whether the way in which the worker manages his or her work affects the amount of money the worker makes.

- Whether the worker also carries out work for other people.

For example:

- A groom who works 5 days a week for one person, has to start work at 7.30 a.m. every day, is told what yard work to do and which horses to exercise, will almost certainly be seen as an employee.

- On the other hand, someone who visits the yard once a week to carry out paddock maintenance using their own mini tractor and who also works for several other yards is more likely to be considered self-employed.

There are many situations in between these examples but in such cases it will be safer to consider the worker as an employee. Although the requirements of employment law will be explained in greater detail later in this chapter, some of the main differences in terms of legal rights between an employee and a self-employed worker are:

- A self-employed worker cannot claim a redundancy payment or unfair dismissal.

- A self-employed worker is not entitled to receive statutory sick pay or maternity leave.

- Income Tax and National Insurance Contributions (NICs) are deducted from an employee's wages by the employer, under the Pay As You Earn (PAYE) scheme. A self-employed worker will be responsible for making their own arrangements for paying income tax and NICs.

- An employer is liable for **torts** (wrongs such as negligence) committed by their employees, but not those of self-employed workers.

The importance of correctly defining a worker as an employee or self-employed can be demonstrated by the following examples:

Example 1   An employer treats a worker as being self-employed and does not therefore operate a disciplinary procedure before dismissing the worker. In such a case the worker could bring a case before an Employment Tribunal claiming that he or she had in fact been an employee and was therefore entitled not to be unfairly dismissed.

Example 2   An employer treats a worker as self-employed and does not therefore deduct tax or National Insurance Contributions from payments made to the worker. In such a case, if HM Revenue and Customs decided that the worker had actually been an employee, the employer might be required to pay HM Revenue and Customs the tax and National Insurance Contributions that should have been deducted from the employee's wages.

ITQ 83 Give another term for:

a. Statute law

b. Common law

ITQ 84

a. Where are civil law cases heard?

b. Where are criminal law cases heard?

ITQ 85 Who generally prosecutes criminal law cases?

ITQ 86 If an individual brought a case against their employer before the courts, what terms would be used to describe the two parties?

The employee:

The employer:

ITQ 87 Besides the 'employer' and the worker, who else might take an interest in whether the worker is an 'employee' or self-employed?

ITQ 88 List some of the factors that might be considered when determining whether a worker is an employee or self-employed:

EMPLOYMENT LAW

You might become an employer in two ways:

1. By taking someone on to work for you in your business.

or:

2. By taking over an existing business that already has employees.

Once you become an employer, you will have to comply with various pieces of legislation, so it is better to have some understanding of these before you embark on this road.

TRANSFER OF UNDERTAKINGS (PROTECTION OF EMPLOYMENT) REGULATIONS 2006

If taking over an existing business, you will have to comply with the Transfer of Undertakings (Protection of Employment) Regulations 2006 (which replace the 1981 regulations). Under these regulations a transfer of an undertaking is defined as occurring when there is a 'transfer of an economic entity that retains its identity', i.e. when a business is sold or otherwise transferred, except where the transfer is only of shares (as in a takeover bid).

The regulations, commonly known as **TUPE**, protect the rights of all employees employed by the business immediately before it was transferred. All of the rights and obligations existing under the employee's contract of employment with the previous employer transfer to the new employer when the business is transferred.

If the new employer does not provide comparable overall terms and conditions of employment, the employee could have grounds for legal proceedings against the new employer.

Specific implications of the TUPE regulations will be covered in greater detail as we discuss the implications of the Employment Rights Act 1996 and other requirements of employment law.

THE EMPLOYMENT RIGHTS ACT 1996

When deciding to take on a new employee, the employer must consider the various requirements of The Employment Rights Act 1996. Key issues are outlined below.

Statement of Terms of Employment

One of the requirements of this Act is that the employee must, unless employed for less than 1 month, be given a written **Statement of Terms of Employment** within 2 months of starting work. In practice it would be better to provide this as soon as the employee starts work and even to have the main points of it drafted before starting to recruit.

Prospective employees will want to know what will be required of them, and the terms and conditions against which they would be employed should their application be successful. On the other hand, you will almost certainly want to make interviewees aware of certain conditions before deciding to take them on.

The Employment Rights Act 1996 requires that the following are included in the Statement of Terms of Employment:

- The names of the employer and employee.

- The date the person started employment.

- The continuous service date. This might not be the same date as the particular employment started – the employee may have worked for the employer in a different capacity immediately prior to this employment (e.g. as a trainee), or the employee may have worked for the company before the employer took over the business (see TUPE).

- Rate of pay (see also National Minimum Wage).

- Frequency of pay (whether the person will be paid weekly or monthly).

- Hours of work (starting and finishing times, hours per day/week).

- Holiday entitlement (including public holidays) and holiday pay.

- Conditions relating to incapacity for work because of illness or injury, including sick pay provisions.

- Pensions entitlement – which must also state whether contracted-out from the State Earning Related Pension Scheme (SERPS) – this will be explained in the section dealing with PAYE and NICs). Although the statement of terms must state what the employee's pension entitlement is, this may in fact be nothing. However, the employer does have to make pension arrangements for employees in line with legislation passed in October 2001 if there are more than 5 employees in the business. In such cases, the employer must offer a **stakeholder pension** to the employees, but does not have to make employer contributions. The statement of terms should also make it clear whether a company pension scheme is in place.

- The job title (a job description is not essential but may be useful).

- Place of work.

- When the job is not permanent, the period of time for which it is expected to continue or, if for a fixed term, the date that the job finishes.

- Notice period.

- Disciplinary rules and grievance procedures.

- Details of any collective agreements with Trade Unions which affect the employment.

- Details relevant if the employee is required to work outside the UK for more than 1 month.

The Statement of Terms of Employment might also be referred to as a 'Statement of Particulars of Employment' or a 'Statement of Terms and Particulars of Employment'.

Although the Employment Rights Act allows some of the details (e.g. full disciplinary and grievance procedures) to be given in a separate document, it is usually easier for the small employer to give all the information in one document.

ITQ 89 Besides taking on a new employee, in what other way might you become an employer?

ITQ 90 What is the intention of the Transfer of Undertakings (Protection of Employment Regulation) 2006?

ITQ 91 Name the Act which requires an employee to be given a Statement of Terms of Employment.

ITQ 92 How long after the employee starts work does the employer have in which to give the employee a Statement of Terms of Employment?

ITQ 93 When would an employer not have to give the employee a Statement of Terms of Employment?

ITQ 94 When would be the best time to draft the Statement of Terms of Employment?

Once the terms have been agreed between the employee and employer, and the statement of terms issued, any changes must be put in writing within 1 month of the change. Any changes in the terms must be agreed between the employer and employee. *The employer cannot change the employee's terms without the employee's agreement.*

If an employer does not give an employee a Statement of Terms of Employment, the legislation allows the employee to make a complaint to an Employment Tribunal. The Employment Tribunal will then state what the terms are. The employee in such a case would not be entitled to any compensation and the employer would not be liable to pay any form of fine. Even so, the Statement of Terms of Employment serves a useful purpose in that it leaves both parties in no doubt as to what the terms are.

For example: After working for an employer for 6 months, the employee's work is proving to be unsatisfactory and the employer has decided to terminate the employment. The employee is paid monthly, in arrears. The employer did not give the employee a written Statement of Terms of Employment. In such a case, the employee could argue that he or she was entitled to 1 month's notice although the minimum statutory notice period in such circumstances would be 1 week. The employer could have avoided confusion and uncertainty as to the employee's rights by including a term within a Statement of Terms of Employment, limiting the notice period to the statutory minimum.

An employer may also wish to use the Statement of Terms of Employment to record the employee's agreement to terms and conditions beyond those required by the Employment Rights Act and other legislation. This might include:

● The employee's agreement to having a medical examination if required in support of claims for sick pay.

● The employee's agreement to a confidentiality clause – this may be required by the employer if the employee has access to confidential information which might, for instance, be useful to a competitor. Such a clause might specify a period of time beyond the end of the employment in which the employee is bound not to disclose confidential information.

ITQ 95 How can an employee's terms of employment be changed?

ITQ 96 What timescale is allowed for confirming changes to an employee's terms in writing?

Protection against Unfair Dismissal

Under the Employment Rights Act 1996, an employee must not to be unfairly dismissed and must receive written reasons for dismissal.

In certain cases, some employees with less than 1 year's continuous service are protected from unfair dismissal. These cases would include when the main reason for dismissal was:

● Union related – for instance if the employer dismissed the employee for joining (or even refusing to join) a union.

● Related to health and safety – for instance if the employer dismissed the employee for refusing to carry out a task which contravened health and safety legislation.

● Related to the employee asserting a statutory right – for instance not to have certain deductions taken from their wages.

● For a maternity-related reason – for instance, an employee taking time off to attend ante-natal classes.

- Related to the effect of the Working Time Regulations – for instance an employee refusing to change their working hours to exceed 48 hours per week.

Employees with continuous service of more than 1 year, dismissed for one of these reasons, would also have a claim for unfair dismissal as they are held to be automatically unfair.

If an employee is considered by an Employment Tribunal to have been unfairly dismissed, the employer will normally be required to pay financial compensation to the former employee.

The figure to be paid will be made up of:

- **A basic award** – calculated (according to the age of the employee) as up to one and a half times the employee's gross weekly wage (up to a specified maximum), multiplied by the number of years of continuous employment (up to a maximum of 20). Note that the figure for the maximum weekly wage is index-linked and therefore changes. (If you take over an existing business, remember that the length of continuous service of employees who worked for the business prior to you taking it over will, because of TUPE, include *all of the years* they have worked for the business – not just the years they have worked for you.)

- **The compensatory award** – to compensate the employee for the loss suffered because of the unfair dismissal. The employee is, however, under a duty to keep losses to a minimum, which usually means he or she should look for other work. The Employment Tribunal takes into account whether the employee has found other work and, if so, at what wage rate. However, if the employee has not found any other work, the tribunal will form a view as to how long he or she is likely to remain unemployed and will base their calculation of the compensatory award payable on this. There is a cap on compensatory awards which changes from time to time.

If an Employment Tribunal considers that an employee was unfairly dismissed, they can also require that the employee is given back their job or given another job in the same organization. In practice, this rarely happens and the employer is much more likely to have to pay financial compensation.

For an employer, the process of defending a tribunal claim can involve legal fees, management time and a negative effect on the morale of other employees on top of any financial award, so it is important to take professional advice if such a situation arises.

Reasons for fair dismissal and further information regarding unfair dismissal claims and how you can avoid them are discussed later in this chapter.

CONSTRUCTIVE DISMISSAL

An employee might also have grounds to claim unfair dismissal if forced to leave their job through the unreasonable behaviour of their employer. This is known as **constructive dismissal**.

ITQ 97 After what length of continuous service does an employee usually have the right not to be unfairly dismissed?

ITQ 98 List the reasons for dismissal that would be seen as unfair even if the employee had less than 1 year's continuous service:

1.

2.

3.

4.

5.

Statutory Minimum Notice Period

Under the Employment Rights Act 1996 an employee has the right to be given at least the statutory minimum period of notice as follows:

- One week's notice for an employee who has been employed for 1 month or more but less than 2 years.

- Once employed for more than 2 years the employee becomes entitled to 1 week's notice for each year of continuous service up to a maximum of 12 weeks after continuous service of 12 years.

SUMMARY DISMISSAL

However, an employee is not entitled to any notice if guilty of gross misconduct. Dismissing without notice is sometimes referred to as **summary dismissal**. What acts constitute gross misconduct is open to interpretation and an employer can therefore risk an unfair dismissal claim and a claim for financial compensation for losses by dismissing an employee without notice.

An employer who considers that an employee is guilty of gross misconduct must act quickly – if not, the delay in acting might be seen as evidence that the employer did not consider the conduct to be that bad.

For example:

A livery client sees an employee disciplining a horse in an over-zealous manner. The client, concerned about such an act, reports the employee to the employer. Whilst it may seem obvious that such an act constituted gross misconduct, this would depend on:

- The speed with which the matter was dealt with. If the employee was allowed to continue working for the rest of the day with no mention of the incident and then dismissed on the grounds of gross misconduct at the end of the day, such delay may be seen as condoning the act.

- Whether the employer usually condoned such practices but was dismissing the employee purely because the client had witnessed it.

If an employer does not give the correct notice to an employee, the employee can claim financial compensation for wrongful dismissal. This would be calculated as the loss to the employee in terms of the pay and benefits (for instance keep for their horse or personal accommodation) that would have been received during the notice period, but wasn't. As with compensation for unfair dismissal, the employee must take all reasonable steps to minimize their losses (technically known as **mitigation**). This would usually be taken to mean trying to find new work.

ITQ 99 Explain the following terms with regard to compensation for unfair dismissal:

a. Basic award

b. Compensatory award

ITQ 100 What would be the statutory minimum notice period for the following employees?

a. An employee dismissed after 18 months of continuous service.

b. An employee dismissed after 6 years of continuous service.

ITQ 101 What is 'summary dismissal'?

Statutory Sick Pay

Employees have rights, under the Employments Rights Act 1996, to Statutory Sick Pay (SSP). The mechanics of calculating and paying Statutory Sick Pay (SSP) will be covered later in this chapter. It is however important for the prospective employer to understand that employees might be entitled to SSP if they are off work because of illness or injury and that in most cases the employer may only be able to claim back a proportion of this from the Government. The financial implications of this could be very significant to a small business.

Other Requirements of the Employment Rights Act 1996

Other requirements of this Act include:

- That the employee must receive an itemized payslip.

- The right for the employee not to have deductions (other than PAYE and NICs) to which he or she has not agreed taken from the wages.

Issues relating to paying staff are dealt with in more detail later in this chapter.

THE EMPLOYMENT RELATIONS ACT 1999

The Employment Rights Act 1996 has in certain areas been amended by the Employment Relations Act 1999. The main points of this legislation that will affect the equestrian business are:

- Additional maternity leave provisions.
- Rights of leave for adoptive parents.
- The right to parental leave.
- Rights for part-time workers.

The Act also covers several points regarding trade union membership and collective bargaining procedures for organizations employing more than 20 workers. Although many of these provisions will not be relevant to most equestrian businesses, the Act prohibits employers from discriminating on the basis of membership or non-membership of a union.

Maternity and Adoption Rights

The Employment Rights Act 1996, as amended by the Employment Relations Act 1999, gives employees the right to receive Statutory Maternity Pay (SMP) and to take maternity leave.

All employees, regardless of their length of service, have a right to:

- Time off for ante-natal care. This must be paid at the employee's normal rate of pay. It may include relaxation and parent-craft classes as well as medical examinations.

- Protection against detrimental treatment or dismissal on the grounds of pregnancy or childbirth.

- Ordinary maternity leave of 26 weeks duration.

In addition to the rights outlined above, employees are also entitled to take an additional 26 weeks maternity leave after the period of ordinary maternity leave has ended. This can allow the employee to take a total of 52 weeks leave.

Employees may, if they meet certain requirements, also be entitled to up to 39 weeks Statutory Maternity Pay. This is usually paid at the rate of 90% of the employee's salary for the first 6 weeks and then at a specified rate for the remaining 33 weeks. Those who do not qualify may be entitled to Maternity Allowance (MA).

The financial implications of SMP to the employer are minimal – at least 92% of the SMP paid out is reimbursed to the employer by the Government. For a small employer (those whose total NICs for the previous tax year are less than a specified amount) 104.5% of SMP payments are reimbursed. This should enable the small business to take on temporary staff to cover the gap left by the employee on maternity leave, but may not compensate for an experienced member of staff's absence for a prolonged period.

Employees can opt not to take their full allowance of maternity leave, but at least 2 weeks leave after the baby is born is compulsory. This is extended to 4 weeks for factory workers and can be extended further under Health and Safety Regulations.

Statutory Adoption Leave is available for up to 52 weeks, with Statutory Adoption Pay (SAP) for up to 39 weeks.

ITQ 102 Why might an employee's entitlement to Statutory Sick Pay have a significant effect on a small business?

ITQ 103 What maternity rights do employees have, regardless of their length of service?

ITQ 104 What would qualify as ante-natal care?

ITQ 105 What is the minimum amount of maternity leave that an employee must take?

ITQ 106 In what way are the financial implications of Statutory Maternity Pay less onerous to the small business than the financial implications of Statutory Sick Pay?

Parental Leave

In addition to maternity/adoption leave, the Employment Relations Act 1999 allows both parents to take up to 13 weeks parental leave for each child. (If both parents work for the same employer, they are both entitled to parental leave but the employer may request that they do not take the leave at the same time.) The employee does not have to be paid for any period of parental leave taken.

Leave can only be taken to care for a child, but this may include time off simply to spend more time with the child in his or her formative years. Leave can be taken at any time up to the child's fifth birthday or, if adopting, within 5 years of the date of placement for adoption. Parents of disabled children may be able to take the leave up to the child's 18th birthday.

This right applies to both full-time and part-time staff but note that 'one week' is seen as the normal length of time the employee would work in the week. For instance, if an employee usually worked for 2 days per week, 'one week's leave' would be the 2 days normally worked.

Employees must have completed 1 year's continuous employment to qualify for parental leave. To qualify for the leave, the employee must either be named on the child's birth certificate or must have been given legal parental responsibility for the child, e.g. have adopted or been appointed as the child's legal guardian.

Employers and employees can arrange between them the details of how parental leave should work. In the absence of such an agreement, the **'Fallback Scheme'** developed by the Government will apply. This allows:

- Leave to be taken in blocks of between 1 and 4 weeks (except for parents of disabled children, who can take leave in longer or shorter blocks).

- For employees to give at least 21 days notice of their intention to take parental leave to the employer.

- For the employer to postpone the parental leave by up to 6 months, (by written notice within 7 days of receipt of the application for leave) if he or she considers that business would be unduly disrupted if the employee were to take leave when requested. The employer cannot, however, postpone the leave if the employee wishes to take it immediately following the birth or adoption of the child.

ITQ 107 How many weeks parental leave are parents allowed to take?

ITQ 108 If both parents worked for one employer, which would be entitled to parental leave?

ITQ 109 What conditions must be met for an employee to qualify for parental leave?

1.

2.

Employees have the right not to be treated unfairly or to be dismissed because they take, or seek to take, parental leave and could take their employer to an Employment Tribunal if they considered this to be the case.

Other Leave

In addition to parental leave, employees also have the right to reasonable time off to deal with an emergency relating to a dependant e.g. if a child or spouse has an accident or is taken ill. Unlike many of the other rights of employment, this right exists from the first day of the employment. The amount of time off allowed is limited to that necessary to deal with the immediate crisis and make arrangements for long-term care. The employee would not, for instance, be allowed to take several weeks off to care for a child with chicken pox. Payment for such time off is at the discretion of the employer, but the employee must not be dismissed or victimized for taking the time off.

The rights outlined above are the minimum required by law.

Part-time Workers

The main point of the Employment Relations Act 1999 as regards part-time workers is that it gives the Secretary of State authority to introduce measures to prevent discrimination against part-time workers in terms of their employment rights.

The terms and working conditions for a part-time worker should be no less favourable than those of their full-time colleagues. This means that part-time workers must have at least the same contractual rights as comparable full-timers in terms of pay, holidays and pensions. These may, however, be adjusted pro-rata, e.g. a part-time worker working half the hours of a full-time worker might reasonably expect to get half the amount of pay or holiday in the same period as the full-time worker.

Permission to Work in the UK

In recent years there has been a large change in the migration of workers internationally, with many overseas workers seeking employment in the United Kingdom, and this places additional responsibilities on prospective employers. It is important that potential employees provide proof of identity (such as a UK passport). However, if the individual is a migrant worker then the appropriate authorities should be consulted as, under the Immigration, Asylum and Nationality Act 2006, there are penalties for employing illegal migrant workers.

NATIONAL MINIMUM WAGE REGULATIONS 1999

The National Minimum Wage Act 1998 became law on 1 April 1999. It was amended in 2003 to ensure that an enforcement notice can be served on an employer whether or not the employee is still in employment. HM Revenue and Customs is responsible for enforcing the regulations.

The requirements of the Act do not apply to:

- The self-employed.
- People under 18 years of age.
- People working and living as part of a family.
- Apprentices under the age of 19 years.
- Apprentices over 19 years of age in the first 12 months of their apprenticeship.

The minimum hourly rates of pay set by the Act are divided as follows:

- A general minimum wage.

- A minimum wage for workers under 18 years old who are not of compulsory school attendance age.

- A minimum wage for workers aged 18–21.

- A minimum wage for workers over 22 years old.

The rates change periodically so you must check them. Contact the Employer's Help Line on 0845 6000678.

Employees are entitled to see pay records if they have good reason to suspect they are not being paid the minimum wage. Employees can make a complaint to an Employment Tribunal or a civil court if their employer does not produce pay records or is paying less than the minimum wage. Additionally, HM Revenue and Customs can instigate criminal proceedings for non-compliance with the requirements of the Act.

WORKING TIME REGULATIONS 1998

The Working Time Regulations (WTR) came into force on 1 October 1998. The regulations implement the requirements of the European Working Time Directive. The regulations limit the hours an employee can be required to work and set minimum requirements in terms of rest breaks, days off per week and entitlement to annual holiday.

Under the WTR, workers cannot be required to work more than an average of a 48-hour working week by an employer. The employee can, however, choose to work more than an average of 48 hours if he or she wants to, but this agreement must be in writing and may be rescinded by the employee at any time.

Other provisions of the regulations are that:

- Night workers cannot be required to work more than an average of 8 hours in 24.

- Night workers also have a right to free health assessments.

- Workers have a right to 11 hours rest per day.

- Workers have a right to one day off each week.

- Workers have a right to an in-work rest break if the working day is longer than 6 hours.

PAID ANNUAL LEAVE

The Working Time Regulations also set a required minimum amount of paid holiday that must be given to an employee. Employees are entitled to 5.6 weeks paid holiday per year (28 days if a 5-day week is worked).

The easiest way to administer this is to decide for your employees when the 'leave year' will start. For instance, you might decide that the year in which the employee can take their leave entitlement runs from January to December or perhaps September to August.

When an employee starts work or leaves within a leave year, the overall holiday entitlement for that 12-month period will be calculated on the basis of the proportion of the year worked.

There is no statutory requirement for workers to have leave on public holidays and where an employee is paid for public holidays, these may be included within the statutory 5.6 weeks leave.

ENFORCEMENT

Several bodies have responsibility for enforcing these regulations. Employment Tribunals will enforce the entitlements to rest periods and breaks – though the Arbitration and Conciliation Service (ACAS) can be used to arbitrate in the early stages of a dispute. The Health and Safety Executive (HSE) and local authorities will enforce the working time limits.

ITQ 110 To whom do the requirements of the National Minimum Wage Regulations not apply?

1.

2.

3.

4.

5.

ITQ 111 What could happen to an employer who does not comply with the National Minimum Wage Regulations?

ITQ 112 Under the Working Time Regulations, what is the average maximum number of hours an employee can be required to work in a week?

ITQ 113 Under what circumstances can the employee work more than the maximum required number of hours per week?

ITQ 114 List the main provisions of the Working Time Regulations in terms of rest breaks:

1.

2.

3.

ITQ 115 How much paid annual leave is an employee entitled to as a minimum?

ITQ 116 Who is responsible for enforcing the different aspects of the Working Time Regulations?

1.

2.

EQUAL OPPORTUNITIES

Laws are in place to ensure that all members of society have equal opportunities with regard to employment. The laws prohibit discrimination (unfair treatment based on prejudice) in society as a whole on the grounds of:

- Race
- Sex
- Marital status
- Disability
- Trade union membership
- Age

The main Acts of Parliament regarding equal opportunities and discrimination with which you must comply when recruiting and selecting staff are:

- The Race Relations Act 1976.
- The Sex Discrimination Acts 1975 and 1986.
- The Disability Discrimination Act 1995.
- The Employment Relations Act 1999.

- The Equality Act 2006.
- Employment Equality (Age) Regulations 2006.

Discrimination on grounds of race, sex, marital status, disability, trade union membership or age is illegal at the interview and selection stages of recruitment, and during employment while selecting people for promotion or redundancy, as well as in the day-to-day interaction of staff. The main provisions of the law regarding discrimination because of trade union membership are that the employee should not be discriminated against on the grounds of either belonging or not belonging to a union.

The law on discrimination applies to all employees and to contract labour (e.g. temporary staff).

Defining Discrimination

Direct discrimination is when someone treats another less favourably than he or she treats or would treat another person, on grounds of race, sex, marital status, disability or union membership. For example, if an advert stated that only women should apply for a job as a groom, this would be direct sexual discrimination against any man who applied for the job.

Indirect discrimination is where a condition of employment would make it more difficult for a person of a specific race, sex, etc. to comply with the employment terms than for other people. Such cases may be seen as indirect discrimination.

For example, if an advert stated that the successful candidate for a job as a groom for event horses must weigh less than 50 kg (about 8 st), this might be seen to discriminate indirectly against men as they would, as a generality, find it more difficult to comply with this term.

A term that might be seen as indirect discrimination would, however, not be seen as such if the employer could demonstrate that it is a justifiable requirement of the position, regardless of the employee's sex, race, etc. For instance, if the employee would be required to school show ponies or ride yearlings and two-year-old racehorses, the maximum weight would be a justifiable requirement of the position.

Remedies for Discrimination

An Employment Tribunal can award unlimited compensation for loss of earnings, prospective loss of earnings and injury to feelings for direct discrimination.

For indirect discrimination, they can recommend that the employer takes action to avoid the effect of discrimination, and that this action be carried out within a specified period.

- **Positive discrimination** (favouring one group: either racial or sexual) is generally unlawful.
- **Positive action** (promoting equality of opportunity) is legal and could include placing job advertisements in the media aimed at minority ethnic groups, or providing a workplace nursery.

Racial Discrimination

The Race Relations Act 1976 defines racial discrimination as discrimination on the grounds of colour, race, nationality, or ethnic or national origins. The Commission for Racial Equality is charged with the duty of eliminating racial discrimination. They can help an individual prepare and present a case to an Employment Tribunal.

EXCEPTIONS

An exception to the requirement to comply with racial discrimination legislation exists where belonging to a specific racial group is a genuine occupational qualification for the job (e.g. an actor playing a role or someone working in a restaurant from a particular region). No such circumstances will apply to equestrian businesses, so racial discrimination in such businesses will always be illegal.

Sexual Discrimination

The major pieces of legislation relating to sexual discrimination are the Equal Pay Act 1970 and the Sex Discrimination Acts 1975 and 1986. The Equal Opportunities Commission is the main body offering assistance and advice in this field, fulfilling a similar role to the Commission for Racial Equality.

As well as making discrimination on grounds of sex unlawful, the Sex Discrimination Act also makes it illegal to discriminate on grounds of marital status.

EXCEPTIONS

Discrimination is not illegal if the potential employee would be living or working in a private home – for example working as a nanny/groom, or a live-in groom. In such cases it is lawful for the employer to specify a preferred sex. It may also be lawful to employ people of the same sex in a small business (6 persons or less) under some circumstances, but professional advice should be sought before pursuing this policy to ensure its legality.

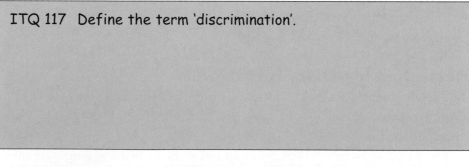

ITQ 117   Define the term 'discrimination'.

ITQ 118   What is 'direct discrimination'?

ITQ 119 What is 'indirect discrimination'?

ITQ 120 What is the difference between positive discrimination and positive action?

Discrimination on Grounds of Disability

The law regarding discrimination on grounds of disability is governed by the Disability Discrimination Act 1995.

Although the Act does not force 'small businesses' (those with less than 15 employees) to comply with these regulations, it would be good practice to ensure that employment arrangements do not discriminate against the disabled.

The Act makes it unlawful to discriminate against disabled people 'unjustifiably'. In practice, this means that you cannot discriminate on grounds of disability if the person's disability is irrelevant to the employment. Nor can you discriminate against a disabled person in terms of employment if a reasonable adjustment to terms of employment or facilities would make such discrimination unnecessary.

What constituted 'reasonable adjustment' would take into account the following factors:

● The effectiveness of any adjustment in taking away the disadvantage to the disabled person.

● How practical the adjustment would be to make.

● How much it would cost to make the adjustment and how much disruption it would cause.

● The financial resources available to the employer.

● The availability of financial assistance to the employer.

As with all legislative requirements, you must seek professional advice from a solicitor or the Employment Service regarding the specific circumstances should such circumstances arise.

EQUINE BUSINESS MANAGEMENT

ITQ 121 When would it be legal for an employer to discriminate on the grounds of sex?

ITQ 122 How many employees must a business have before it has to comply with the requirements of the Disability Discrimination Act 1995?

ITQ 123 When might a business with more than the specified number of employees legally be able to decide not to employ a disabled person?

ITQ 124 What factors would be considered in deciding whether an employer's decision relating to not employing a disabled person was reasonable?

1.

2.

3.

4.

5.

Age Discrimination

The Employment Equality (Age) Regulations 2006 outlaw unjustified age discrimination in employment. Under the regulations an employer cannot discriminate on grounds of age in recruitment procedures, unless a certain age range is a genuine occupational requirement (GOR) for the job. The circumstances in which age will be a GOR are uncommon. It is not unlawful to request a candidate's date of birth, but an employer must be careful not to use this information to discriminate.

The Employment Equality (Age) Regulations 2006 has removed the upper age limit for entitlement to claim unfair dismissal. Previously, the Employment Rights Act 1996 stated that only employees under the age of 65 years with 1 year's continuous employment had the right not to be unfairly dismissed.

THE CONTRACT OF EMPLOYMENT

A Contract of Employment is a legally binding agreement between the employer and the employee. It can consist of some written terms (e.g. the Statement of Terms of Employment) and some terms agreed verbally (e.g. at interview). In fact, if the employer neglects to put any terms in writing, a contract based entirely on verbal agreement can still exist. However, as with all contracts, it is preferable to ensure that major terms are agreed in writing. This will make it much easier to prove what was actually agreed at a later date if necessary.

The Contract of Employment should be drafted before recruitment. This will enable the employer to make sure that the prospective employee is aware of all of the terms and conditions of employment before taking the decision to employ them. Likewise, it will give the prospective employee the opportunity to decide not to go ahead with the application if some of the terms and conditions were not to his or her liking.

CONFORMING TO STATUTORY REQUIREMENTS

The Contract of Employment will almost certainly include the details of the Statement of Terms of Employment required by the Employment Rights Act 1996. It may expand upon these and could also include other conditions.

The terms of employment agreed in the Contract of Employment may *exceed* the legislative employment requirements but cannot take away any of the employer's or employee's statutory rights, even if they have agreed to it. For example, the Contract of Employment might allow the employee to take more than 5.6 weeks paid holiday a year (the minimum decreed by the Working Time Regulations) but could not legally state that less than 5.6 weeks would be paid, even if the employee agreed.

Alternatively, the Contract of Employment might allow more than 13 weeks parental leave to be taken (as required by the Employment Relations Act) or might allow the employee to take parental leave after the child's fifth birthday. It could not, however, legally state that the employee agreed to forego their rights to parental leave.

Another example would be that the Contract of Employment could not legally specify a lower rate of pay than that specified in the National Minimum Wage Regulations, even if the employee agreed to work for less.

A Contract of Employment cannot be changed by the employer unilaterally. Changes to an employee's terms and conditions of employment can only be brought about by agreement between the employer and employee.

Some of the terms and conditions of an employee's contract may not be contained within the Contract of Employment itself but within another document referred to within it.

DISCIPLINARY PROCEDURES

As mentioned earlier in this chapter, the Statement of Terms of Employment provided to the employee under the requirements of the Employment Rights Act 1996, should include the disciplinary procedures and grievance procedures in place.

Commencing in 2004 there was a statutory requirement for employers to follow a specific process when conducting disciplinary procedures, with Tribunal awards being as much as doubled in some cases where employers had made even minor procedural errors. The legislation proved to be the most burdensome employment law of all for employers and, rather than reduce Tribunals, which was the original aim, it actually increased them and made them more expensive and this prompted the Government to revise the regulations.

With effect from 6 April 2009 The Employment Act 2008 abolished the statutory requirements, replacing them with the ACAS Code of Practice – Disciplinary & Grievance Procedures (The Code), though there is no legal requirement to follow The Code. The Code places more emphasis on being fair than on the details of disciplinary and grievance procedures, however, it does endorse following the principles laid down in the statutory procedures in order to achieve a fair process.

Although the Act allows for such details to be provided in a separate document, the small employer will probably find it easier to keep all of the conditions within one document.

Wherever the procedure is published, it should be easily understood and practical to follow. It will form part of the employee's Contract of Employment and if you fail to follow it if disciplinary action becomes necessary, your employee could claim you were in breach of contract.

A disciplinary policy usually stipulates that a member of staff will be dismissed only after a given number of verbal and written warnings have not been heeded and responded to in an appropriate fashion.

When dealing with possible disciplinary action it is always prudent to consider:

- Whether the employer could be considered to be in breach of contract.

- Whether the employee could claim unfair dismissal.

- Whether the employee could realistically claim discrimination on the grounds of race, sex, disability, trade union membership or age.

Earlier in this chapter we covered circumstances in which dismissal of an employee would be considered unfair. In order for a dismissal to be considered fair, the main reason for dismissal must be one of the following:

- Unacceptable conduct of the employee (e.g. theft).

- That the employee can no longer meet a legal requirement of the job (e.g. if employed as a driver, losing his or her driving licence).

- That the employee proves to be incapable of doing the job or unqualified to do it (e.g. if someone employed as a groom proved incapable of handling horses).

- Redundancy as a result of the job for which the person was employed effectively disappearing (for instance in a livery yard, if all the livery horses left, there may be no job left to do).

- For some other substantial reason. (We would advise seeking legal assistance in determining validity in such cases.)

In addition to offering at least one of these reasons, the employer must be able to demonstrate that they acted reasonably in deciding to dismiss the employee for that reason and in following a fair dismissal procedure.

Examples of fair procedures include giving the employee a chance to explain their conduct and granting a right of appeal if they choose to exercise such a right. Following a simple disciplinary procedure and documenting the steps taken will help the employer, if necessary, to prove to an Employment Tribunal that they behaved reasonably if dismissal was necessary because of the employee's poor conduct.

Much can be achieved by communicating effectively with staff – an informal chat with an employee can prevent problems arising or escalating in the first place and can address problems that have arisen before the consequences take effect.

For example, a member of staff in your yard is required to muck out all stables each morning, removing all droppings and wet or dirty straw and then bedding down. It comes to your notice that the employee is not mucking out thoroughly enough. In such circumstances, before implementing disciplinary procedures it might be reasonable for you to consider:

- Whether the employee had been made aware of the importance of the method by which the task should be carried out.

- Whether the employee had sufficient time to carry out the task in the required method.

You could have an informal chat with the employee at this point to make them aware of the importance of the method of mucking out and perhaps help them to plan the day more effectively so that the task could be achieved without affecting other tasks to be performed.

Verbal Warnings

As on all occasions where you need to reprimand a member of staff, it is important to ensure that you speak to them in private and that you endeavour to ensure that you will not be interrupted. Belittling a member of staff in front of other employees or clients does little to help long-term staff relations and would reflect badly on you with your clients.

Once the problem gets to the point of a verbal warning being given, you must inform the employee clearly that you are giving them a verbal warning so that they are in no doubt that disciplinary procedures are being implemented. It would also be prudent for you to keep a note of the main points of the conversation, including what the problem is and how long you have allowed for performance to be brought up to a satisfactory level, on the staff file.

You must also ensure that you take steps to monitor the employee's performance after the warning has been given and, at the end of the period allowed, let them know whether or not you are now satisfied with their performance.

ITQ 125 List the three major points an employer should consider before implementing disciplinary procedures.

1.

2.

3.

ITQ 126 Give four reasons for dismissing an employee that would usually be considered fair.

1.

2.

3.

4.

ITQ 127 What else must the employer be able to do in order to demonstrate that the dismissal was fair?

Written Warning

This is a formal warning, a copy of which should be retained in the staff file. As with a verbal warning, the written warning must make it clear what the employee needs to do in order to bring performance to a satisfactory level and detail what time period you will allow for this.

After this time, should the employee's performance still fall below that required, you could reasonably decide to terminate their employment and provide them with such a period of notice as you have agreed in their Contract of Employment.

Staffing records should be held in a secure place, as they are confidential documents. All records of disciplinary matters concerning an individual should be kept on file. This would include written warnings, as well as agreements made between employee and employer to resolve the situation.

Ideally, these records should be signed by both parties to show that they have been received, agreed and understood. When a written warning is given, the employee should be told how long the warning will remain 'on file'. If the employee's performance improves to the required standard during this period the warning should be removed from the employees' staffing record at the end of the period.

BREACH OF CONTRACT BY THE EMPLOYER

If an employer is in breach of contract, i.e. fails to comply with the Terms of Employment agreed, the employee can claim financial compensation (damages) for losses reasonably incurred because of the breach. As mentioned earlier (Unfair Dismissal) the employee would be required to take steps to mitigate losses.

The most common breach of an employment contract by an employer is the failure to give an employee full contractual notice when the contract is terminated.

We have already mentioned the minimum statutory notice period that must be given and that the Contract of Employment may give the employee greater rights than the statutory minimum. If the Contract of Employment stated that 1 month's notice would be given, even if the statutory notice period applicable was only one week, the employer would be in breach of contract if failing to give the employee the full *contractual* notice.

ITQ 128 What is a Contract of Employment?

ITQ 129 What might the Contract of Employment consist of?

ITQ 130 Why would it be better to agree all terms and conditions of employment in writing?

ITQ 131 What can a Contract of Employment do and not do in terms of an employee's statutory rights?

PAYING STAFF

You will have agreed a rate of pay within the Contract of Employment for your employee and the interval at which payment will be made. If you have agreed an hourly rate, multiply it by the number of working hours in the pay period to calculate the gross pay. You might alternatively have already agreed a weekly or monthly rate that can be used as the gross pay for the period. If this is the case, you must ensure that the corresponding hourly rate meets or exceeds the National Minimum Wage Rate.

Weekly payments to staff are usually called **wages**. When paid monthly, payment is referred to as a **salary**.

The employee must be provided with a **written pay statement** (an itemized payslip) giving details of the gross amount, all deductions (see below) and the take home pay. (As mentioned earlier, provision of a payslip showing all deductions is a requirement of The Employment Rights Act 1996). The payslip will be produced automatically by the computer if you use software with an integrated payroll.

STATUTORY DEDUCTIONS AND CONTRIBUTIONS

Having decided to take on staff, you need to find out your main obligations in respect of **Pay As You Earn** (PAYE) and **National Insurance Contributions** (NICs).

- PAYE is a method of collecting and paying over to the Tax Office income tax that is due on an employee's earnings.

- NICs, based on the employee's wage, are paid by both the employer and employee. (NICs are also paid by the self-employed.)

The employer deducts the employee's contributions from their wages and pays this over, together with the relevant employer's component of National Insurance contributions, to HM Revenue and Customs. In consultation with your accountant you need to devise the best method of arranging for staff to be paid and contributions calculated. There is a range of computer software which automatically calculates deductions once the employees' tax codes have been entered. Alternatively you can use the services of a specialized payroll agent or computer bureau. The majority of employers leave calculation of PAYE and NICs to the accountant.

The Lower Earnings Limit

You do not have to operate PAYE and NICs if all of your staff earn below the Lower Earnings Limit (LEL) for National Insurance and thus below the rate at which PAYE is payable. However, if any of your staff have another job elsewhere or have a BR or K tax code (see Tax Codes later this chapter) you will have to operate PAYE and NICs regardless of the employee's earnings for that member of staff.

When you need the information, find out from HM Revenue and Customs what the current lower earnings limit and PAYE threshold is.

Note that, since taxation and contributions levels change periodically, no set figures will be quoted within this text.

GETTING STARTED

If any of your staff will earn more than the LEL amounts, or are working for you as a second job, you must inform your local Tax Office. They will then tell you what your tax collection reference number is and send you an **Employer's Starter Pack**. The Starter Pack will include all of the paperwork necessary to calculate and submit contributions.

Other leaflets such as Employers' Bulletins may also be enclosed. It is important that you read through these as they often contain instructions on how to implement recent changes such as those detailed in a recent Budget Speech. Most computer accountancy packages containing an integrated payroll will be automatically updated by the software supplier in line with changes in taxation.

ITQ 132 When would you have to operate a PAYE account for your staff?

TAKING ON NEW STAFF
National Insurance (NI) Number

HM Revenue and Customs' National Insurance Contributions Office provides a NI number to all employees who are liable to NICs so that NICs can be correctly recorded on each person's National Insurance account. As soon as an employee starts work you should ask them for their NI number. If the employee does not know their number it should be on their P45 (see below). Information is also given below regarding the employee who does not have a P45. It is possible to trace NI numbers through any Social Security or PAYE Tax Office.

The P45

On the new employee's first day, ask for the P45 which would have been issued to them by their last employer. This is a multi-part form completed by an employer when an employee leaves. *Note that you will have to provide a completed P45 whenever an employee leaves your business.* When a new employee gives you their P45 it should already have had Part 1 (the front yellow coloured sheet) detached and sent to the Tax Office. Part 1A (the second blue sheet) should also have been detached and retained by the employee. If this is still attached, hand Part 1A back to the employee.

You should be given Part 2 (green sheet) and Part 3 (pale blue sheet).

1. Check that the tax code (item 5) and the tax week/month, total pay to date, and total tax to date (item 6) on Part 3 of the form are the same as those written on Part 2 of the form. If not, contact your Tax Office immediately for instructions.

2. If Items 5 and 6 on Parts 2 and 3 of the form agree, your accountant can prepare a Deductions Working Sheet (P11) for the new employee.

3. Complete Part 3 of the P45 and send it immediately to the Tax Office.

4. Keep Part 2 of the P45 on file for at least 3 years after the end of the tax year it relates to.

The P46

In general, if a new member of staff could not give you a P45 (they may not have had one or may have lost it), you will need to fill out a form P46 to let the Tax Office know that this person is now working for you. The P46 is fairly self-explanatory and includes sections for the employee and employer to complete. In case of difficulty, consult your local Tax Office.

There are exceptions to this procedure:

- Students – ask the Tax Office for a copy of the *Employer's Further Guide to PAYE and NICs* (publication code CWG2) and follow the instructions under 'Students'.

- If the employee will be working for you for less than 1 week, consult the Tax Office for advice.

Send the completed P46 to the Tax Office and complete a Deductions Working Sheet (P11). Be advised by the Tax Office as to which tax code to use whilst you are awaiting notification of the employee's tax code from the Tax Office.

Tax Codes for PAYE

Everyone is allocated a tax code by HM Revenue and Customs. Tax codes consist of numbers and letters and are used to calculate the amount of tax payable by the employee for each pay period. The numbers in the tax code are the first three figures of the employee's tax allowance (the amount that can be earned in the tax year without paying income tax on it). For instance, a member of staff whose tax allowance is the personal allowance only (equal to the Lower Earnings Limit of £6,475 in 2009–2010) would have a tax code starting with the figures 647. The letters in the tax code show how the allowance has been made up and how it should be altered if changes in the Budget are announced. By using an integrated payroll system on a computer you should have up-to-date tax codes as the software supplier updates the packages as necessary.

Where a new member of staff has not provided a P45 and you have completed a P46, the Tax Office will (within a few weeks, hopefully) provide a tax code notification to you. In the meantime, use the tax code advised by the Tax Office.

Once you have completed and sent the P45 to the Tax Office and discovered which tax code to use for your new employee, the next step is to notify your accountant or wages secretary. When using computer software with an integrated wages roll, depending on the type of software, what generally happens is that the tax code and gross pay are entered and the computer calculates the deductions.

Everyone is entitled to earn a certain amount tax free. The taxable income at the time of writing (June 2009) taxed at 20% is up to £37,400 per annum. 40% tax is payable on the excess over £37,400. The rates of income tax change periodically in the Budget so bear this in mind at all times.

Example:

If an employee is paid £12,000 per annum the tax payable in one year (at current rates) is calculated as follows:

Gross:	12,000
Tax free:	6,475
Taxable:	5,525
Tax @ 20%	(5,525) x 20% = 1,105
Total tax due	**1,105**

Find out the following current figures:

a. The single person's allowance

b. The normal rate of income tax

NATIONAL INSURANCE CONTRIBUTIONS

Class 1 NICs	are payable on employed earners' wages. They comprise employer's contributions and employee's contributions.
Class 2 NICs	are payable by the self-employed at a flat rate.
Class 3 NICs	are voluntary payments that are made by people wishing to help qualify for a retirement pension. They may be paid by those not working or those not paying enough Class 1 or Class 2 contributions to qualify for a state pension.
Class 4 NICs	are payable by the self-employed based on the amount of net profit made.

NICs for the Self-employed

Self-employed people must (unless eligible for exemption) pay Class 2 National Insurance contributions at a flat rate per week. Class 2 contributions count towards Incapacity Benefit, the State Pension, Widow's Benefit and Maternity Allowance.

In addition to this, Class 4 contributions will also be payable if your profits are above a set lower limit. Contributions payable are calculated as a percentage of the profits above the specified lower limit and below the specified higher limit.

ITQ 133 Which parts of the P45 should a new employee give you?

ITQ 134 What is it important to check on the P45?

ITQ 135 Having checked the information on the P45 and found it to be incorrect, what should you do?

ITQ 136 If the information on the P45 is correct, what should you do next?

1.

2.

ITQ 137 When would you need to complete a P46?

ITQ 138 What class of National Insurance Contributions are paid by employed workers?

PAYING PAYE AND NICS TO HM REVENUE AND CUSTOMS

Payments can be made quarterly to HM Revenue and Customs if the combined total PAYE and NICs due for a month are less than £1,500. For most small businesses it may be better to pay smaller amounts more often to lessen the effect on cash flow.

Payments must be received by HM Revenue and Customs by the 19th (by post) or 22nd (electronically) of each month for the previous tax month (ending the 5th of the month). The Payslip Booklet (P30BC) includes a payments slip for each tax month. This must be completed and paid in at a bank or sent to HM Revenue and Customs by post.

At the front of the booklet is a summary page where you can record the total amounts of NICs and PAYE payable for the month and any amounts of SSP and SMP recovered (see later this chapter).

End of Year Returns

At the end of each tax year you will need to complete an End of Year Summary (P14) for each employee for whom you have deducted PAYE and NICs.

First complete the End of Year Summary at the bottom of each P11 and then simply transfer the information to the P14. The P14 is a three-part form. The top two copies are for HM Revenue and Customs, one for tax and one for

National Insurance. The third part is a form P60. This should be handed to current employees as a record of their total NICs and PAYE deductions for the tax year.

An Employer's Annual Return (P35) is then completed and sent with HM Revenue and Customs' copies of the P14s to HM Revenue and Customs. The final date for submission of the Annual Return is 19 May – penalties are payable for late submission.

STATUTORY SICK PAY

As mentioned previously, employees have a right, under the Employment Rights Act 1996, to receive **Statutory Sick Pay (SSP)** for periods of sickness qualifying for payment.

Period of Incapacity for Work (PIW)

In order to qualify for payment of SSP, the employee must have been sick for a period of at least 4 days in a row – this is known as a **Period of Incapacity for Work (PIW)**. There is no legal requirement to pay staff for sickness periods of less than 4 days unless you have specified to the contrary in the employee's Contract of Employment.

The 4-day period is 4 calendar days, i.e. a member of staff who is sick on Friday, Saturday, Sunday and Monday will qualify even if they normally only work Monday to Friday.

LINKING PIWS

PIWs (each of 4 days or more) which are separated by less than 56 days (or 8 weeks) are linked and treated as one PIW. For example, Jane Brown is sick from 17 to 23 November 2009 (7 days) and then from 11 to 15 December 2009 (5 days). She would have had two PIWs separated by less than 8 weeks: these two PIWs would therefore be linked and treated as one PIW of 12 days.

If however, the two periods were more than 8 weeks apart, they would be treated as separate PIWs. If one of the periods was for less than 4 days, it would not qualify as a PIW and would not therefore be linked with the other period, even if both occurred within the 8-week period.

NOTIFICATION

An employee must notify you that they are sick in order to qualify for SSP. You can specify in the Contract of Employment within what time period the employee should notify you that they are sick. For SSP purposes you *cannot* insist that the employee:

● Notifies you in person.

● Notifies you earlier than the first qualifying day (e.g. for a Monday to Friday worker who becomes sick on the Saturday, you cannot insist that they notify you before Monday – their first qualifying day).

● Notifies you by a certain time on the first qualifying day.

- Uses a special form for notifying you.

- Updates you on their progress more than once a week.

- Produces a medical certificate as notification.

However, if you have not stated anything regarding notification within the Contract of Employment, the employee must ensure that you are notified within 7 days of the first day of the PIW.

It is possible to withhold payment of SSP if the employee delays in notifying you and there appears to be no good reason for doing so. It would be best, however, to check with the Benefits Agency before taking this course of action.

EVIDENCE

The employee must also provide evidence of their incapacity in order to qualify for SSP. Your employee must be told what evidence of incapacity you would expect them to produce.

NHS doctor's sick notes are not available for sickness periods of 7 days or less. You may therefore ask an employee to write a short statement concerning their sickness (this is called **self-certification**) for sickness periods of up to 7 days and that they provide a **Doctor's Certificate** for periods of more than 7 days.

You must decide whether, on the basis of the evidence provided, you consider that your employee is incapable of work and therefore eligible for SSP. A Doctor's Certificate should normally be accepted as evidence provided you do not have strong evidence to the contrary – for example a groom certified sick with a bad back seen competing in a local Hunter Trials!

If you consider withholding SSP on the basis of evidence, it is recommended that you seek the advice of your local Benefits Agency before doing so.

PAYING SSP

A specified flat rate is payable per week to employees with average weekly earnings exceeding the specified minimum. Once you have decided that the employee is eligible for and should be paid SSP, your accountant will calculate the amount of payment and record it on the P11.

RECOVERING SSP

More often than not, an employer cannot claim back from the State the SSP he or she has paid. The only time that you may be able to do this is if the SSP represents more than 13% of the total NICs (employers and employees contributions) that you, the employer, are due to pass over to HM Revenue and Customs for that tax month.

This amount would be deducted when making the monthly payment of PAYE and NICs to HM Revenue and Customs.

ITQ 139 What is the minimum number of days sickness to qualify for payment of Statutory Sick Pay?

ITQ 140 What term is used to describe a period of sickness qualifying for payment of Statutory Sick Pay?

STATUTORY MATERNITY PAY

Employees taking Ordinary Maternity Leave may be entitled to receive Statutory Maternity Pay (SMP) for this period (up to 39 weeks).

To qualify, the employee must have completed at least 26 weeks continuous service with her employer by the 15th week (the qualifying week) before the expected week of childbirth. Also, for the 8 weeks before the qualifying week, she must have had average weekly earnings of more than the Lower Earnings Limit for NICs.

Period of Maternity Pay

The **Maternity Pay Period** may start at any time after the start of the 11th week before the expected week of confinement. If the employee continues working until the baby is born, the Maternity Pay Period will start from the Sunday following the date of the baby's birth.

RECOVERING SMP

All employers can recover 92% of the SMP they have paid out. Small businesses (defined as those whose total NICs in the last tax year were less than the specified threshold) can recover 100% of the SMP paid plus 4.5% extra to cover additional costs.

GENERAL STAFF RECORDS

It is good practice to open a file for each individual member of staff as they are taken on. This will allow all relevant records to be kept together, making it easier for you to refer to them when needed. Most staff records will be confidential and it is therefore important to ensure that access to staff files is restricted.

In general, staff files will include records such as:

- The signed Contract of Employment and any agreed changes to it.
- Copies of pay statements.

- The employee's P45.
- Details of staff appraisals (if these are carried out).
- A record of holidays and sickness.
- Training details.
- A record of disciplinary action and grievances.

Staffing records should be kept for at least 2 years after the end of the employment as they may be required as evidence at any Employment Tribunal to demonstrate that the employer had behaved reasonably.

CHAPTER SUMMARY

In all dealings with staff and prospective staff, the employer must ensure that he or she complies with current legislation and can demonstrate that this is the case. The information given in this chapter is aimed at providing a general understanding of the principles of employment law – it is not intended as a substitute for professional legal advice and should not be used as such.

Employment legislation is constantly being created and updated. Increasingly, UK law is complemented by or superseded by EEC law, such as the Working Times Directive. The employer in an equestrian business has to keep up to date with these regulations in order to ensure that employees are being treated fairly and to avoid the possibility of paying heavy fines or compensation. Employers have found to their cost that their employees have rights too – including the right not to be discriminated against and to receive a reasonable wage.

This chapter has provided basic information on issues such as PAYE, NICs, Statutory Sick Pay and Statutory Maternity Pay. As with other matters covered this book, changes in laws and Government policy mean that these aspects of employing staff are constantly changing. If, at any time in the future, you need to operate a PAYE account, for example, make sure that you obtain current guidance and information from HM Revenue and Customs and consult your accountant.

In the next chapter we discuss the important topic of health and safety at work.

CHAPTER 6

HEALTH AND SAFETY FOR THE EQUESTRIAN BUSINESS

The aims and objectives of this chapter are to explain:

- The general obligations of employers and employees under the Health and Safety at Work Act 1974.

- How to carry out risk assessments within the equestrian business.

- The main principles of the Manual Handling Regulations 1992 (as amended).

- The main principles of the Control of Substances Hazardous to Health Regulations 2002 (COSHH) (as amended).

- The implications of the Personal Protective Equipment (PPE) at Work Regulations 1992 (as amended).

- The principles of employee training.

- How to write a health and safety policy statement.

- What is involved in Reporting of Injuries, Diseases and Dangerous Occurrences Regulations 1995 (RIDDOR).

- The insurance requirements of the business.

THE HEALTH AND SAFETY AT WORK ACT 1974

The requirements of the Health and Safety at Work Act 1974 cover the employer, the employee and all visitors to the business premises. The legislation is enforced by the Health and Safety Executive (HSE) and, in some situations, local authorities.

All employers have a legal responsibility to ensure the health and safety of their employees so far as is reasonably practicable. The Health and Safety at Work Act 1974 compels employers to maintain safe equipment, premises and procedures.

Whilst it is beyond the scope of this chapter to discuss the Act fully, everyone involved in a professional capacity with horses should be familiar with their responsibilities under the Health and Safety at Work Act. Up-to-date information should be obtained from the Health and Safety Executive website www.hse.gov.uk which contains some excellent, free to download, information leaflets.

GENERAL RESPONSIBILITIES

Under the Health and Safety at Work Act 1974, employers and employees have the following general obligations:

- Employers must ensure the safety of their employees by maintaining safe systems of work, safe premises and safe equipment.

- Employees and self-employed persons must take reasonable care to avoid injury.

- Employers, employees and the self-employed must not endanger the health and safety of third parties.

- Employers must ensure that all employees and others are instructed and trained in the jobs they have to do and in the use of all equipment.

- A named person must be specified, to whom any hazards or faults in equipment can be reported.

- Employers must ensure that their insurance covers all persons on the yard and the use of all equipment.

- All employers must have Employers' Liability Insurance and the certificate must be displayed.

- An 'Appointed Person' to deal with first aid and a well-equipped first aid kit should be available.

RISK ASSESSMENT

It is a legal requirement for all businesses to conduct risk assessment. If there are 5 or more employees within the business then risk assessment must be recorded. It is important to understand that risk assessment is a straightforward concept based on common sense, along with your knowledge of the job. It should not be made over-complicated.

Risk assessment is simply the process of:

- Identifying hazards in the workplace.
- Assessing the likelihood that a hazard will cause harm (its risk).
- Determining the potential severity of the harm.
- Determining ways of reducing or eliminating the risk.

Every employer is required to make a 'suitable and sufficient' assessment of:

- **The risks to the health and safety of the employees whilst they are at work.** Employees are considered to be 'at work' all the time they are on the premises, even when they are not actually working – for example when they are on a tea break, or have not yet left for home at the end of the day. They are also 'at work' when they are off the premises, but working – for example escorting a hack. The term 'employees' covers temporary workers and trainees/working pupils as well as those who are normally employed. (An exception is equine studies or other students on a course of study, who are not considered to be employees of their college.)

- **The risks to the health and safety of people not in employment arising out of or in connection with the running of the business.** All clients and visitors (college students, riders, farriers, vets, helpers, etc.) have to be considered as well as employees.

- **The risks to their own health and safety if they are self-employed.** For example, instructors who visit their clients' yards, and those teaching freelance for an equestrian centre. These risk assessments should cover risks to their own health and safety, and those of their clients.

HOW TO ASSESS RISKS

1. **Look for the hazards.** A hazard is anything that can cause harm; falling off a horse, being trodden on or kicked and damaging your back whilst lifting bales of hay or bedding are all hazards. Most aspects of handling horses and many aspects of yard work present a hazard of one sort or another. Other hazards can be identified by reading manufacturers' instructions for any equipment used, looking in the accident book to assess the most commonly occurring accidents, and walking around the yard looking for areas where accidents are likely to occur. Trivial hazards, like paper which might cause paper cuts during filing, can be ignored in a risk assessment.

2. **Identify who might be harmed, and how.** Trainees, young, new or inexperienced workers and expectant mothers may all be at particular risk, so may maintenance workers, visitors, etc. who may not be in the workplace all the time and have little experience of horses. Members of the public or people who are on the yard but not employed there, such as the people coming for lessons or owners of horses kept at livery, also have to be considered.

3. **Evaluate the risks and decide whether the existing precautions are adequate or whether more should be done.** Each hazard should be considered in terms of whether the risk is high, medium or low, the severity of harm it could cause and if there is anything that can be done to reduce the risk. Can the hazard be eliminated? If there are any additional precautions that need to be put in place an 'action list' should be drawn up and priority given to the risks which are highest or could affect most people.

CONTROLLING RISKS

In controlling the risks the following principles should be applied, in this order:

1. Try a less risky option (e.g. using a wheelbarrow to move bales of hay rather than carrying them yourself).

2. Prevent access to the hazard (e.g. put a grille on the stable door of a horse who bites).

3. Ensure all personnel are correctly trained in carrying out the procedure.

4. Organize work to prevent exposure to the hazard.

5. Issue personal protective equipment.

6. Provide welfare facilities (e.g. washing facilities, an area for staff to take breaks and a first aid kit).

Methods that may improve health and safety in a riding establishment might include placing a mirror where the horses exit to the road if there is a 'blind corner' in order to prevent road accidents, and ensuring that surfaces, particularly steps and ramps, are made of non-slip material. A 'no smoking' policy, fire signs, and fire protection in high-risk areas, such as stores, are basic requirements.

ITQ 141 Complete the sentences.

Risk assessment is the process of:

1. Identifying ....

2. Assessing ....

3. Determining ....

REVIEWING RISKS

Having assessed the risks, they should be recorded and then reviewed periodically. Risk assessments should be revised if there is reason to suspect that they are no longer valid, or there has been a significant change in the work process, equipment, location, layout or personnel involved.

If changes to an assessment are required then they should be made as soon as possible. Risk assessments are required to be 'suitable and sufficient', not 'perfect.'

In summary, the risk assessment should show that:

- A proper check was made.
- All the people who could be affected were considered.
- Obvious hazards that could be eliminated were dealt with.
- The precautions are reasonable and the remaining risks are low.

Summary of the Risk Assessment Procedure

1. Record the location or activity covered by the assessment, and the reason for the assessment, along with all the individuals taking part in the process.

2. Record any business activities, tasks and equipment that could reasonably be expected to cause harm to people. Identify any specific hazards associated with each as appropriate.

3. Record the individuals at risk and rank the level of risk – low, medium or high. This ranking helps to determine the level of action to be taken.

4. Determine whether existing controls are adequate or if further action needs to be implemented.

5. Review recommended actions to be taken and record that action was taken as appropriate. Prioritize for action items that could have a high level of risk as well as those that could affect a number of people.

6. Communicate all findings to employees.

7. Identify any training needs and review assessment as necessary.

An example of a risk assessment record sheet is given on page 140. The likelihood of the incident occurring and the potential to cause harm are allocated points. These points are added together to give a final rating for the risk.

RISK AREAS IN A STABLE YARD

Most stable yards will contain a number of potential risks, the chief of which include:

1. **Combustible materials**. Stables, hay barns, oil, diesel and petrol storage areas are high-risk areas. Electric, gas or oil heaters, bonfires and electrical wiring all present hazards.

2. **Electrical equipment**. Clippers, grooming machines, kettles, etc. Under the Electricity at Work Regulations 1989 many electrical items must be inspected periodically by a qualified electrician and have a sticker showing the date of the appliance test. This includes extension leads – in order to find out which pieces of equipment need testing, and when, visit the HSE website (see page 133) and look for information regarding 'Portable Appliance Testing'. A residual current device (circuit breaker plug) should always be used with high-risk electric equipment such as clippers and grooming machines. Equipment should be checked for damage such as cracked casings or stresses caused by friction.

3. **Barley/linseed boiler**. If gas-powered, the boiler must be positioned away from any flammable material. If electrically powered it must be checked as mentioned above. Display signs warning of the danger of hot barley or linseed – it can burn the employee and the horse!

4. **Horse-walkers**. These must be well maintained in accordance with the manufacturer's instructions. The area must be enclosed and the machine must only be operated by trained personnel.

5. **Tractors and all terrain vehicles (ATVs)**. Those driving the tractor or ATV should be trained in the safe use of the vehicles and have passed the relevant tests. Particular attention must be paid to the dangers of working on steep slopes, near ditches, rivers and power cables. A suitable crash helmet must be worn when using an ATV. Passengers should not be permitted in the hay/muck trailer.

6. **Horse box and trailers**. The driver must check that people and animals are not close to the lorry or trailer when manoeuvring. The lorry ramp must be well maintained to make sure it is easy to close. If the springs are worn or the ramp is simply very heavy, there is a danger of back injury to those closing it. The ramp must not be of a design that can lower without restraint to the ground.

7. **Steps and stairs**. These must be well maintained, well lit and a handrail provided. Apply salt to prevent them becoming slippery in icy conditions.

8. **Ladders and steps** must also be well maintained and be strong enough for the job. Ladders must never be left up as they can be knocked down and cause injury, or encourage children to climb them. Untrained junior personnel must never use ladders unsupervised. When in use, the ladder must be securely propped, with the base secured on a non-slippery surface to prevent it slipping.

RISKS WHEN HANDLING HORSES

All practical skills involved in the handling and management of horses should be included in the risk assessment.

Task	Risk to handler	Control measures
Moving around yard.	Trips and falls, slipping on ice.	Keep yard clear of baler twine, tools, etc. Put down salt in icy conditions.
Handling horses, grooming, rugging, tacking up.	Bite, tread and kick injuries. Fingers caught in lead rope.	Train handlers. Tie horse up, wear stout footwear, never kneel next to horse, never put hand on the ground near horse. Never entwine fingers in lead rope when tying horse up. Teach horses good manners.
Leading horses, turning out, catching horses in field.	Bite, tread and kick injuries. Rope burns if horse pulls away, squashed between horses.	Train handlers. Wear crash cap, stout footwear, gloves. Horse to wear a bridle for leading. Never entwine fingers in lead rope or metal rings of headcollar. Never take bucket of food into field to catch horse(s). Teach horses good manners.
Clipping.	Bite, tread and kick injuries. Electrocution.	Train handlers. Tie horse up, wear stout footwear, never kneel next to horse, never put hand on the ground near horse. When clipping have assistant, use circuit breaker plug, remove water buckets, check clippers and extension lead, rubber matting on floor. Restrain horse adequately. Clippers and extension lead checked periodically in line with the Electricity at Work Regulations 1989.
Lungeing.	Kick injuries, horse pulling away – rope burns.	Train handlers using quiet horses. Wear stout footwear, gloves and crash cap. If trained to an appropriate standard, horse to wear bridle with side-reins attached to increase control. Never allow untrained persons to lunge young or untrained horses.
Riding in enclosed space.	Falling off, kick injuries from another rider's horse.	Train riders. Wear crash cap. Check tack for safety. Teach riders about safety distances. Use horses suited to riders' abilities.
Riding in open spaces and on roads.	Horse bolting, horse shying into passing vehicle, falling off, kick injuries from another rider's horse.	Avoid riding on road. Box to off-road area. Train riders – never allow novices out of enclosed area. Never take traffic-shy horses on the public road. First, try to overcome fear of traffic in a controlled environment. Wear bright, reflective clothing and crash cap, safe riding footwear.

Riding in open spaces and on roads (cont.)	Horses get more excited when out of the arena.	Teach riders about safety distances. Make sure horses wear suitable bits. Use horses suited to riders' abilities and get all riders to train for and take the BHS Riding and Road Safety test.
Loading and unloading into and out of lorry or trailer.	Kick, crush and tread injuries. Rope burns.	Train handlers. Wear crash cap, gloves and stout footwear. Horse to wear bridle or chifney, especially if known to be a bad loader. Keep area clear of debris, equipment, etc. Use a loading ramp and bay if available.
Fill in the blanks boxes with other tasks to be assessed.		

Sample handling tasks for risk assessment

This list covers a broad range of handling tasks. There will be other tasks connected to specialist yards such as handling stallions and assisting with the covering procedure at a stud.

ITQ 142 Write down three ways of controlling the risks identified in the risk assessment:

1.

2.

3.

RISK ASSESSMENT

Location or activity covered by this assessment:

Lungeing a young horse in the outdoor school

Persons involved in carrying out the task and level of training	Under 18-y-o (trainee)	Never to be done by under 18-y-o
	Employees	Sandra Green - PC 'A' Test holder
	Non-employees	
	Others (specify)	

Reason for assessment	Tick	Personnel involved with this assessment
Initial assessment		
Work process change		N Smith - Yard Manager
Equipment change		
Location change		
Layout change		
Personnel change		
Annual assessment		

Potential to cause harm	5	Negligible	Slight	Moderate	Severe	Very severe
		1	2	3	4	5

Details: Young horse is more likely than a trained horse to kick handler or pull away.

Details of any control measures already in place which will reduce the hazard:

Horse lunged in enclosed arena, wearing side-reins, if appropriate. Handler well-trained and experienced.

Personal protective equipment: Crash cap and gloves. Stout footwear.

Taking into account present control measures, what is the likelihood of a risk occurring?	2	Assessment rating (high, medium or low)	5 + 2 = 7 = medium Assessment Ratings: 10 = High 9 = High 8 = High 7 = Medium 6 = Medium 5 = Medium 4 = Low 3 = Low 2 = Low
Very likely	5	**Details:** As handler well-trained and safe equipment used, risk is	
Likely	4	medium. Untrained person never to lunge young horses. As horse's	
Quite possible	3	training improves, risk becomes lower.	
Possible	2		
Unlikely	1		

Signatures of personnel involved with this assessment:	N. Smith	Date: 05.03.10 Date:

Sample of a risk assessment form

PROCEDURES FOR SERIOUS AND IMMINENT DANGER AND FOR DANGER AREAS

Where a serious risk could arise in the event of an accident or vandalism, plans should be made for what people should do. Every business has to consider the possibility of fire, but this is particularly important in the equestrian industry where many businesses are storing large volumes of flammable substances such as hay and straw, and often storing them, and horses, in wooden (and therefore also highly flammable) buildings.

Other potentially dangerous situations that need to be considered are accidents with horses when being handled (clipping, boxing, shoeing) or when under saddle. The person responsible should establish appropriate procedures to be followed whilst potentially dangerous procedures are carried out, as well as procedures for when things go wrong.

This person should organize which staff are responsible for implementing procedures such as the evacuation of the premises, filling in the accident book, etc. These appointed staff should also ensure that none of the employees have access to any area to which it is necessary to restrict access on grounds of health and safety, unless the employee concerned has received adequate health and safety instruction.

For example, it could be a yard manager's job to ensure that the staff for whom he or she is responsible know which animals on the yard are particularly difficult to handle, and to prevent the less experienced from carrying out procedures such as clipping these animals until they are competent. On the same basis, a stud manager might delegate stallion handling to a particularly experienced member of staff, and mare management to others, because the stallion could be more of a risk to the health and safety of the employees than could the mares.

The employer must inform staff of:

- The risks to their health and safety identified by the risk assessments.
- The preventive and protective measures.
- The procedures for accidents and emergencies.
- The identity of those persons nominated to carry out the procedures.

MANUAL HANDLING

The Manual Handling Regulations 1992 cover the minimum health and safety requirements for the manual handling of loads where there is a risk, particularly of back injury, to workers. These regulations are clearly directly relevant to people working 'hands on' in the equestrian industry. Moving sacks of feed, barrows of manure, bales of hay and straw, and manipulating horsebox and trailer ramps are all examples of manual handling.

The regulations require each employer to 'avoid the need for… employees to undertake manual handling operations at work which involve a risk of their being injured, as far as it is reasonably practicable to do so'. In practice this means ensuring that work routines are carefully considered in advance. Is it possible to use a winch to lift soaked haynets rather than dragging them out by hand? Where can you site the muck heap to minimize risk of injury, and how will you manage it? Putting in a ramp and banking the sides of the muck heap, rather than having one huge mound, can make unloading barrows easier as well as looking much tidier.

Where it is not reasonably practicable to avoid the need for employees to undertake any manual handling operations at work which involve a risk of their being injured, the regulations require each employer to:

● Carry out a risk assessment for all manual handling operations to be undertaken by staff.

● Reduce the risk of injury to those employees doing any manual handling operations to the lowest level that is reasonably possible.

● Provide employees who are undertaking manual handling with information about the loads that they have to carry.

● To review (and where necessary change) risk assessments regularly and when circumstances change.

Where the regulations impose duties on employers for their employees, those duties are also imposed on self-employed persons (who have a statutory duty to look after themselves). Therefore, if you run your own yard, even if you do not employ anybody else, you should still carry out risk assessments. Your duties to yourself are as high in the eyes of the law as an employer's duties to his or her employees. Though you may decide that you are prepared to work without regard for the legislation, in theory you could be prosecuted for failing to do so, just as employers could be prosecuted for failing to take the health and safety of their employees into account.

In order to reduce the risk of injury, the manual handling risk assessment might identify the following possibilities:

● The yard layout could be improved to make manual handling safer or less strenuous. Perhaps the feed room could be sited closer to the stables.

● The amount of twisting and stooping could be reduced. Perhaps the feed could be dispensed from hoppers rather than out of bins on the ground.

● Repetitive jobs could be minimized. Automatic drinkers could be installed, or, if all the horses receive the same mix, one container could be pushed once round the yard and the feed dispensed from that, avoiding the need for many trips with buckets.

● Obstructions can be moved or re-sited.

● Loads can be made lighter or easier to grasp, perhaps by buying from different suppliers.

- A sack barrow can be provided for moving awkward-shaped loads such as bales of shavings and paper.

- Lighting can be improved.

- Training can be provided.

EMPLOYEES' DUTIES

Employees are required to make 'full and proper use of systems of work provided for their use by their employers while at work.'

In practice this means that employees have to:

- Co-operate with their employers on health and safety matters.
- Use equipment provided for their safety.
- Follow the systems of work that have been laid down for their safety.

So, in order to comply with the regulations, if an employer puts in a winch for lifting wet haynets, the employees are obliged to use it.

MANUAL HANDLING RISK ASSESSMENTS

Any task involving manual handling must be assessed in the same way as all other tasks and areas of work are assessed. For example, in the case of moving a heavy load, the following need to be assessed:

- **Is there a risk of injury?** Try to decide if the task could result in injury.

- **Is it reasonably practicable to avoid moving the load?** In many cases you cannot avoid having to move the load.

- **Is it reasonably practicable to automate or mechanize the operation?** If so, for example if a forklift is to be used to move bales of hay or shavings, a new risk has to be considered.

If you or an employee are contemplating moving a load you must assess whether or not you are physically capable of doing so. If you know you cannot lift a full feed sack or bale of shavings, it would be foolish to attempt to do so. Estimate the weight of the load and, if necessary, seek help.

Having decided that you do have to move the load and that you are physically capable of moving it, bear in mind the following points:

- Wear gloves to ensure you will have a secure grip. When moving hay bales wear gloves to protect your hands from the twine.

- Stand close to the bale or sack with your feet apart to help you maintain balance.

- Square the sack up in front of you.

- Keep your spine straight and bend your knees – don't lean over the sack to lift.

- Lift by straightening your knees rather than using arm strength alone.

- Keep your arms close to your body and keep your chin tucked in.

- Heavy items should be moved on a sack barrow rather than being carried, and assistance should be sought where possible.

- When carrying water buckets make sure the buckets are evenly filled and not too heavy. It is better to carry two buckets half full than one bucket completely full. This way you stay balanced with the weight evenly distributed and are therefore less likely to twist or strain your back.

- When putting heavy items down, remember to bend your knees, not your back.

- If moving hay from a stack, always take bales from the top – never pull out the lower bales as the stack may collapse.

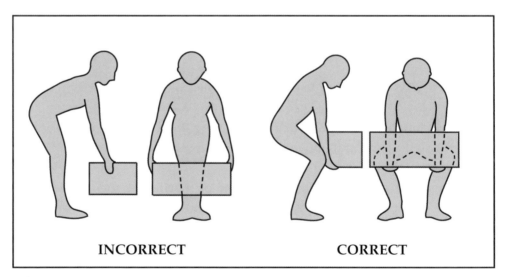

INCORRECT   **CORRECT**

Lifting technique

THE PROVISION AND USE OF MANUAL WORK EQUIPMENT

Equestrian businesses provide equipment in the form of pitchforks, shovels, hoists, clippers, saddlery, horse transport, etc. These can cause injury if used incorrectly or badly maintained. The employer therefore has obligations to ensure that:

- The risks of using the equipment are considered in the risk assessments where appropriate.

- Correct procedures for using the equipment are incorporated into the health and safety policy where appropriate.

- The equipment is well maintained and as safe to use as possible.

- Staff know how to use the equipment correctly, or are provided with training and supervision.

- Staff know what to do and who to notify if they find a fault in an item of equipment.

ITQ 143 Under the Manual Handling Regulations 1992, what is the main requirement of the employer?

ITQ 144 List some ways of minimizing the risk of injury while lifting and moving a bale of shavings.

CONTROL OF SUBSTANCES HAZARDOUS TO HEALTH (COSHH)

The 2002 COSHH regulations contain many sections, not all of which are relevant to employment in the equestrian industry. However, in this section we shall consider some that are.

CATEGORIES OF HAZARDOUS SUBSTANCES
Substances hazardous to health can be divided into three main categories.

Hazardous Substances Used Directly in Work
These include:

- Stored items that may be flammable, such as petrol, cleaning or painting liquids.

- Poisons – for example chemical sprays used for estate management such as fungicides, pesticides, rodenticides, herbicides or fertilizers.

- Anthelmintics (wormers), all veterinary drugs, topical agents, antiseptics and disinfectants.

- Substances carrying a warning label. This would include preservatives such as wood stain.

- Any other substance which creates a hazard to the health of any person.

- Asbestos*. This may be found in the fabric of older buildings, including outbuildings and stables.

- Lead*. Can still sometimes be found in old pipes and paintwork.

*Asbestos and lead have their own regulations and are not dealt with under COSHH.

IN-TEXT ACTIVITY

List any other substances found on the stable yard that could potentially be hazardous to health:

Hazardous Substances Arising from the Work

One of the most prevalent hazards in equestrian businesses is dust of any kind, when present at a substantial concentration in the air. Dust is produced when filling haynets, mucking out musty beds/shaking out mouldy bedding (neither of which should occur in a well-run yard) and grooming horses. Sand in a sand school can be blown around and this can be considered a substance hazardous to health. Indoor schools can also be very dusty.

Hazardous Substances that Occur Naturally

This, in the main, means biological agents. It may seem unlikely for an equestrian establishment to expose its employees to biological agents, but a sick horse may have a disease that is transferable to humans, such as ringworm, and may therefore pose a biological hazard. Rats' urine can cause leptospirosis (Weil's disease). Therefore an equestrian employer has a responsibility to carry out a risk assessment in respect of such agents, in order to prevent or control the employees' exposure to risk.

COSHH does *not* apply to biological agents that are not directly connected with the work and are outside the employer's control (such as the cold virus a workmate may be carrying).

PREVENTION OR CONTROL OF EXPOSURE TO HAZARDOUS SUBSTANCES

The COSHH regulations state that: 'An employer must not carry on any work which is liable to expose any employees to any substance hazardous to health unless he has made a suitable and sufficient assessment of the risks created by that work to the health of those employees, and of the steps that need to be taken to meet the requirements of the Regulations.'

Therefore every employer has to ensure that the exposure of employees to substances hazardous to health is either prevented or, where this is not reasonably practicable, adequately controlled.

Where possible, the prevention or adequate control of exposure of employees to a substance hazardous to health should not only or primarily involve the provision of personal protective equipment. Where the assessment shows that it is not reasonable to prevent exposure to a dangerous substance by using an alternative substance or process, the employer must ensure:

- The total enclosure of the process and handling systems.

- That the generation of spills, leaks, dust, fumes and vapours of substances hazardous to health are minimized.

- That the quantities of substances hazardous to health at the place of work are as low as possible.

- That the number of people who might be exposed to substances hazardous to health is as low as possible.

- That eating, drinking and smoking in areas that may be contaminated by substances hazardous to health are banned.

- That suitable hygiene measures including adequate washing facilities and regular cleaning of walls and surfaces are provided.

- The use of suitable and sufficient warning signs for any areas which may be contaminated by substances hazardous to health.

- The safe storage, handling and disposal of substances hazardous to health.

- The use of closed and clearly labelled containers.

However, where the risks are insignificant, the employer is not obliged to act.

Special Control Measures for Health and Veterinary Care Facilities

In veterinary care isolation facilities, where there are horses who are, or are suspected of being, infected with a specified biological agent, the employer should use suitable containment measures to control the risk of infection adequately.

Personal protective equipment that may be contaminated by biological agents should be:

● Removed on leaving the working area.
● Kept apart from uncontaminated clothing and equipment.

The employer should ensure that such equipment is subsequently decontaminated and cleaned or, if necessary, destroyed.

ITQ 145 Name three substances commonly found in the equestrian workplace that could be hazardous to health.

1.

2.

3.

ITQ 146 Give four measures that could be taken to minimize exposure to substances hazardous to health.

1.

2.

3.

4.

Safety Precautions for Herbicide Use

Herbicides are covered by COSHH. All persons using the substances must be trained in their correct and safe use and must be provided with suitable **personal protective equipment (PPE).**

Under the Health and Safety at Work Act 1974 you must conduct a risk assessment for every potentially hazardous procedure and substance on the business premises. Risk assessment is done to enable control measures to be devised and involves identifying the hazard and assessing the following:

1. What are the risks? For example a toxic substance such as a herbicide is poisonous, an irritant and a pollutant. The hazard is the chance of the chemical being ingested, contacted or spilled.

2. Who and what is at risk? For example employees, children, animals, waterways, etc.

3. What is the probability of occurrence of the risk? Is it probable, reasonably probable, remote or extremely remote?

4. Can the hazard be eliminated? Is there a suitable alternative method of weed control?

5. Can the hazard be substituted? Can you use a chemical with less risk?

6. What procedures will reduce the risk? For example, safe storage (see below), protective equipment and training.

7. What training must be given to those using the substance? Can safe systems of work reduce the risk?

8. What warning systems are needed? Signs, instructions and labels are helpful but do rely on human response.

9. What personal protective equipment is needed? Again this relies on a human response – the user must wear the correct and appropriate PPE.

10. What action must be taken in the event of spillage or contact?

The manufacturers of all substances covered by COSHH produce product information sheets giving the exact chemical composition of the product, storage and usage instructions. Detailed information about the action to take in the event of spillage, contact or ingestion is also given.

Every business must have a risk assessment file where records are kept in order. The records must be updated regularly to ensure the assessments are valid and to satisfy the requirements of the Health and Safety Executive. Leaflets on risk assessment and COSHH can be obtained from your local HSE.

IN-TEXT ACTIVITY

1. UK readers: obtain leaflets on COSHH and risk assessment from your local Health and Safety Executive. Overseas readers: obtain the information from an equivalent organization if one exists.

2. Information can be obtained from the HSE website at www.hse.gov.uk

---

STORING HERBICIDES

- Herbicides should be stored in a safe place, i.e. locked away in a secure, cool cupboard or locker.

- The cupboard/locker should be labelled, indicating that hazardous substances are stored within and forbidding access to unauthorized persons.

- Only authorized persons should have access to the locker key.

- Herbicides should always be clearly labelled and stored in their original container.

- Keep herbicides out of the reach of children – remember when actually mixing up and using the herbicide to keep children well away. Put the herbicide away in the locked cupboard as soon as you have finished mixing.

- Store away from food, drink and animal feed.

PROTECTIVE CLOTHING

The person mixing and applying the herbicide should wear protective clothing:

For mixing	For applying through hand-held equipment
Suitable gloves	Suitable gloves
Face shield	Face shield
	Coveralls
	Rubber boots

In the event of a leak, remove contaminated clothing immediately. Wash protective clothing after use.

PERSONAL PROTECTIVE EQUIPMENT

The Personal Protective Equipment at Work (PPE) Regulations 1992 state that it is the employer's responsibility to see that suitable protective equipment is provided to employees free of charge. Many employees will have some of their own protective equipment but it must be made clear to them that if they need any other relevant protective item, it will be provided.

When both handling and riding horses, safety can be improved through the use of appropriate equipment.

- **Crash/skull cap.** The most important item is an approved safety standard crash cap that meets the PAS (Product Approval Specification) requirements. (You need to regularly check the latest safety standards as improvements to headgear are being made all the time.) The chinstrap should be secured before mounting. The crash cap must not have a chin cup, cradle or draw lace. The chinstrap must pass under the jaw and be attached to the harness by a quick-release buckle. Metal hooks should never be used. If borrowing a riding school hat give yourself time to select one that fits properly. Crash caps should be replaced if they sustain a heavy blow as a result of being dropped or involved in a fall. A crash cap should be worn when leading, lungeing and riding.

- **Safety footwear.** Many injuries are caused by horses jumping or simply standing on the handler's foot. Footwear must be water-resistant and stout, preferably with non-slip soles. Flimsy shoes, plimsolls and sandals are not suitable when handling horses. Steel toe caps have caused serious injuries as the steel rim can crush the foot if jumped on by a horse. Therefore the safest type of footwear is stout, thick leather.

  Ideally you should ride in jodhpur boots or long riding boots. These should have smooth soles and small yet defined heels. Wedged soles are dangerous as a foot can become stuck in the stirrup. Trainers also let the foot slip. Wellingtons and walking boots tend to be broad and can trap the feet if they fit too snugly in the stirrup irons. Boots with buckles on the outside can get caught on the side of the stirrup.

- **Body protector.** When jumping, especially for cross-country jumping, a body protector that meets current BETA safety standards should be worn.

- **Gloves.** Gloves are recommended when riding, even in warm weather, as they prevent blisters caused by the rein pressure on the delicate skin between the ring and little fingers. Gloves specifically designed for riding will have reinforced material at this point, but driving gloves are often a suitable alternative. Gloves should always be worn when leading and lungeing horses. Strong rubber gloves must be worn when handling chemicals.

- **Dust masks.** When working in dusty conditions, e.g. when unloading hay or grooming, you may need to wear a dust mask, especially if you suffer from a dust allergy or asthma.

- **Goggles.** If galloping, racing-style goggles will be needed to protect the eyes whilst on the gallops. (A different form of goggles will be needed if using equipment such as a strimmer, blower or angle grinder.)

- **Ear plugs/defenders.** These should be provided for use on the tractor, especially if a noisy type of muck-collecting machine is used.

- **Overalls.** These must be provided to protect from dust, splashing, contamination by rodents, etc.

Safety can also be improved by *not* wearing certain items at inappropriate times.

Jewellery, particularly loop earrings and bracelets, should not be worn when handling horses as these items can become caught, resulting in a ripped earlobe or broken wrist. Necklaces can present a choking hazard in the event of a fall and large rings can become hooked up, (as well as causing considerable damage to a saddle). False fingernails are also dangerous when handling horses as they can be ripped off.

Long hair must always be safely tied back to stop it obscuring your view.

EMPLOYEE TRAINING

The Health and Safety at Work Act 1974 states that employees must receive instruction, training and supervision in order to carry out their job safely. Many accidents at work are caused through lack of skill and experience on the part of the employee. Anyone working with horses, or even simply handling them, should receive thorough training in all aspects of their management. This should involve safety and accident prevention measures.

Inexperienced employees should work under close supervision and under the guidance of an experienced person. The inexperienced employee must not work with difficult or very young horses or be asked to carry out any task for which he or she has not been thoroughly trained.

New members of staff need to receive a health and safety briefing at the start of their employment – this often forms part of the induction. Keep a record of the induction procedure, who was involved and the date(s) on which induction took place. The employee should sign a statement specifying that they have received health and safety induction training. The necessary further training should be planned and documented at this stage.

It is both useful and important to keep records of training given to all members of staff.

> ITQ 147 What is the employer's main responsibility under the Personal Protective Equipment at Work Regulations 1992?

> ITQ 148 List the items of PPE that are relevant to a worker in the equestrian industry:

WRITING A HEALTH AND SAFETY POLICY STATEMENT

By law, any person who employs 5 or more employees must record (write down) the health and safety policy. This is referred to in law as 'a written statement of your health and safety policy'. It is required by Section 2(3) of the Health and Safety at Work Act 1974.

The written statement must include the following components.

YOUR GENERAL POLICY ON HEALTH AND SAFETY

This will be specific to the place of work to which it relates, and will include the significant findings of the risk assessments, and provisions for any group of employees identified by it as being especially at risk. It should state, in simple terms, your general aims with regard to health and safety. This may involve stressing or referring to the following points as appropriate:

- The HSW Act and other relevant safety regulations such as Manual Handling and COSHH legislation.

- The importance of co-operation from the employees and employers and of good communications between the two.

- That neglect of health and safety requirements by staff will be considered as a disciplinary offence.

ORGANIZATION AND ARRANGEMENTS FOR IMPLEMENTING THE POLICY

The primary purpose of the document is to set out an 'action plan' for health and safety, which should include the following elements.

Responsibilities. Define the responsibilities of individuals for carrying out the health and safety policy. Include the job title as well as the person's name to avoid having to update the policy as soon as a member of staff joins or leaves. Names can be updated when the policy is reviewed. The following areas of responsibility should be allocated, and 'deputies' nominated in the event of absence, where appropriate:

- First aid.
- Accident procedures and reporting.
- Fire precautions, fire drill and evacuation procedures.
- Safety inspections of tack, equipment and premises.
- Induction and training.

Systems of work. Describe the specific systems and procedures for ensuring the employees' health and safety. Hazards identified in the risk assessments need to be assessed, and procedures established necessary for the employees to be able to carry out the policy. The employee must have a copy of the risk assessments and be familiar with the safe systems of work detailed. This will include handling and exercising the horses.

Manual handling. Details of manual handling matters will be addressed in the manual handling risk assessments.

Accident recording.	In addition to stipulating to whom the accident should be reported, the policy should state that a full report should be made as soon as possible in the Accident/Incident Book. State where the Accident Book is kept. The locations of first aid boxes must also be stated.
Emergencies and general fire safety.	Describe the action to be taken in the event of a fire.
Electrical equipment.	State who is responsible for organizing the annual inspection of electrical appliances and other guidelines in connection with the use of appliances.
Machinery and equipment.	State who is authorized to give permission to use machinery and who is authorized to use the machinery. Include guidelines for the safe use of machinery.
Tack and saddlery.	Give guidelines as to the employees' responsibility in terms of checking tack for safety. Stress that weak or cracked tack must not be used.
COSHH.	Specify the employees' responsibilities under the COSHH regulations.
Environment and premises.	Details must be given about the standards expected to be maintained in the kitchen and toilet areas and who is responsible for this.
Personal protective clothing.	Specify the employees' responsibilities in terms of PPE.
Occupational health.	Staff should be aware of any occupational diseases such as ringworm, tetanus, leptospirosis, salmonella or farmer's lung.

ITQ 149
a. In terms of staff training, what is induction?

b. What evidence of induction needs to be kept?

ITQ 150 By law, if you employ how many or more employees must you have a written Health and Safety Policy?

Notification of Employees

The Health and Safety at Work Act also states that the policy must be brought to the notice of all employees. Ideally the issues and duties should be discussed with the people concerned in advance, and accepted by them. They will need to have the resources to carry out their responsibilities. The policy should be made freely available to all employees. A copy could be kept in the rest room, or each employee could be given their own copy.

POLICY REVISION

The Act states that the policy should be revised whenever appropriate and every revision must be brought to the employees' attention. Revising the statement will be necessary whenever:

- New hazards are revealed.
- New equipment or working practices are introduced.
- Changes are made in staff duties.
- New regulations are introduced, or existing ones are revised.

Depending on how much the statement has been revised it may be appropriate to either:

- Record and inform staff about the changes only.
- Rewrite and re-publicize the entire policy.

There are no rules about:

- How long the statement should be – it could be one sheet of paper or a thick file or booklet.

- How the statement is set out – as long as all the areas mentioned above are covered.

The written statement does not have to set out your strategy for protecting non-employees, but it is a good idea to address this area in the health and safety policy anyway. Remember: the employer is ultimately responsible under the law for the health and safety of all the employees. The employer should sign and date the completed policy statement.

MONITORING THE POLICY

The effectiveness of the policy should be checked periodically. This can be achieved by:

- Carrying out 'spot checks'.
- Looking in the Accident/Incident Book.
- Asking for comments or reports from senior staff.

Every employer should also:

- Take into account employees' capabilities when they are given jobs to do, with regards to their health and safety. Staff should not be given tasks to do that might result in them getting injured, if they are not competent to carry them out. For example, picking out a horse's hoof incorrectly could result in an accident affecting a person's health and safety, so a trainee should not be asked to carry out this task unless they were competent to do so.

- Ensure that all employees are provided with adequate health and safety training, both on their being recruited, and on their being exposed to new or increased risks.

- Ensure that the training is repeated periodically where appropriate, and adapted to take account of any new or changed risks to the health and safety of the employees concerned.

- Ensure that health and safety training takes place during working hours.

Employees' Duties

Employees have a duty to carry out the health and safety policy implemented by their employer. They should use any protective equipment as required. For example, the health and safety policy of most yards will require the wearing of a crash cap and gloves when handling youngstock or lungeing.

Employees also have a duty to inform the employer if they become aware of anything relevant to the health and safety policy that needs attention.

REPORTING OF INJURIES, DISEASES AND DANGEROUS OCCURRENCES (RIDDOR) REGULATIONS 1995

The most recent RIDDOR regulations were published in 1995. They replaced five sets of previous regulations – so the current regulations are simple by comparison.

No action is required unless there is a reportable accident, dangerous occurrence or case of disease. In which case the following apply:

- If there is a death in the workplace or a major injury, whether the person involved was an employee or not the incident must be reported immediately by telephone, on-line or by email, and a form (F2508) should be completed either with the HSE representative to whom you speak on the telephone, or else submitted within 10 days. Major injuries include:
  – Broken bones, excluding fingers, thumbs and toes.
  – Amputation.
  – Dislocation of the shoulder, hips, knees or spine.
  – Loss of sight (temporary or permanent).
  – Chemical or hot metal burn to the eye, or any injury penetrating the eye.
  – Electric shocks, burns or any other injury leading to hypothermia or

unconsciousness or requiring resuscitation or admittance to hospital for more than 24 hours.
– Acute illness requiring medical treatment caused by eating or inhaling a substance hazardous to health, or as a result of skin contact.

- If there is an accident connected with work that results in an injury that causes the injured person to be away from work for more than 3 days a form (F2508) must be submitted within 10 days. Acts of physical violence causing an absence of 3 days or more should also be reported the same way.

- If an employee suffers from a reportable work-related disease then a form (F2508A) should be submitted. Reportable diseases include:
  – Certain poisonings.
  – Certain skin diseases.
  – Lung diseases, including occupational asthma and farmer's lung (caused by dust inhalation).
  – Infection such as leptospirosis and some others.

- If something occurs which, even though it did not result in a reportable injury, clearly could have done, then whether the person involved was an employee or not the incident must be reported immediately (by telephone) and a form (F2508) must be submitted. Reportable dangerous occurrences include:
  – Collapse or failure of horsebox ramps or floors.
  – Collapse of any buildings.
  – Unintentional explosions.
  – Escape of a substance hazardous to health.

The forms and reports from equestrian businesses should go to the Environmental Health Department of the local authority. For some other types of business the reports should be made to the Health and Safety Executive.

Failure to properly report an accident at work can result in a heavy fine.

Further information, forms, and all current contact details in respect of the above are available from www.hse.gov.uk.

ITQ 151 When should the health and safety policy be revised?

1.

2.

3.

4.

ITQ 152 List as many ways that you can think of to bring a health and safety policy to the attention of the employees.

ITQ 153 How can you monitor whether a health and safety policy is working?

ITQ 154 In terms of the HSW Act, what action should you take if an employee sustains a broken arm whilst at work?

ITQ 155 What does the acronym RIDDOR stand for?

INSURANCE

Every business will need some form of insurance and there are a number of different insurances that need to be considered.

It is sensible to seek the advice of a reputable insurance broker when reviewing insurance requirements. Insurance brokers do not charge fees – they earn their money through commissions received from the insurance companies. It is normal to pay exactly the same whether you go directly to the insurance company or use a broker, so it is sensible to use the expertise of a broker. *Whichever companies or brokers are chosen, it is important to:*

- Check their record for prompt payment of claims.

- Read the small print – check the policies carefully, preferably with your solicitor, to make sure you are receiving the cover you think you are.

- Ensure that your have sufficient cover – insure for full replacement value and consequential loss. If you are under-insured, you will have to pay for the shortfall yourself, which is likely to cause cash flow problems.

COMPULSORY INSURANCE
Employers' Liability

Under the Employers' Liability (Compulsory Insurance) Act 1969, it is a legal requirement of all businesses which employ staff to hold this insurance. It covers legal claims by employees in relation to personal injuries, illness or disease arising out of and in the course of their employment.

Most policies cover for a limit of indemnity of at least £10 million. The Certificate of Employers' Liability Insurance must be displayed at the place of work. By law, the original certificate (or a copy) must be kept for 40 years.

Public Liability

It is essential to have adequate public liability insurance when operating any kind of equestrian business. It covers your legal liability to pay compensation for bodily injury, death or illness caused to a member of the public as a result of defects in the premises, the services offered or negligence by either the business proprietor or staff: £2 million is generally considered to be the minimum acceptable level of indemnity.

As with all insurance, the policy should be read thoroughly. There may, for example, be clauses stating that cover is only valid when the rider is wearing correctly fitted headgear which meets current BSI standards.

Motor Insurance

It is a legal requirement that you are insured against damages if an accident involving your car, commercial vehicle or other vehicle results in the death of or bodily injury to other people, or damage to their property. **Third party insurance** cover is therefore needed on all vehicles and usually includes provision for legal costs such as solicitor's fees.

A **fully comprehensive** policy covers the replacement value of the insured vehicle as well. Vehicles used for hire or reward, such as horseboxes, will be subject to amendments to the policy.

NON-COMPULSORY INSURANCE
Personal Accident

It is important that self-employed persons are covered in respect of financial security in the event of their sustaining a disabling illness or accident. Getting the correct cover, appropriate to individual circumstances, is not that easy to achieve and the clauses of prospective policies should be checked carefully. Employees involved in risky tasks, such as breaking-in youngsters, would be wise to take out a personal accident policy. Although, as employees, they should be covered by Employers' Liability Insurance, in the event of an accident they may only receive limited payments, especially if the accident was not caused by their employer's negligence. One major benefit of being a member of the British Horse Society is that you receive free Personal Accident and Personal Liability cover. It covers you on all your horses but note that it does not provide cover for any type of business activity. It is essential to check specific details with the BHS.

Property and Contents

All buildings should be insured against damage by fire or adverse weather conditions, such as gales or floods. Cover should be based on rebuilding costs and not market value. It is compulsory for all *mortgaged* properties to be insured.

All contents, including tack, should be insured at replacement value. If large quantities of hay and straw are stored, this too should be insured. Most policies have requirements in terms of security of property, e.g. fitting locks and burglar alarms of a certain specification.

Business Interruption

This covers consequential loss of profits as a result of some interruption to the running of the business, resulting from factors such as flood damage, outbreak of disease, etc.

Horses

There is a wide range of insurance policies aimed at the horse owner. Cover can vary from simple third party protection to complete cover including loss of use through disease or injury, mortality, vet's fees and loss by theft or straying, etc.

CHAPTER SUMMARY

Health and Safety law requires employers to use good management and common sense: to look at what risks there are and take appropriate steps to minimize them. These duties apply 'as far as is reasonably practicable'. This means that the law recognizes that some risks cannot be completely overcome – perhaps especially in an area that involves dealing with unpredictable animals such as horses. In other words the degree of risk has to be balanced against the time, cost, physical difficulty and general inconvenience of taking measures to avoid risk. The wearing of crash caps, strong footwear and gloves is a reasonable precaution when dealing with horses; wrapping workers up in cotton wool is not!

As with most other topics covered within this book – make sure that you check current requirements and seek professional advice when required.